NUMEROLOGY

Based on the Vedic Tradition

Everything comes from shunya (zero) and dissolves into shunya

NUMEROLOGY

Based on the Vedic Tradition

Dr. Vinod Verma

Gayatri Books International

Disclaimer

The purpose of this book is to provide knowledge about Vedic numerological astrology. The material provided is for the purpose of education. It is not meant to heal your physical or mental troubles but is intended to initiate you to make an effort for a better life. No claims of any kind will be accepted by the author or the publisher in this direction.

To use the provided information and knowledge in this book for commercial purpose is the violation of the author's intellectual property rights. Violators will be prosecuted.

Visit Dr. Vinod Verma at www.ayurvedavv.com to find out about her other publications and activities like seminars, lectures, consultations, etc. Look for more information on the last pages of the book.

Consultant: Mohit Joshi

Cover design and photographs by the author

ISBN: 978-8189514273

Dedication

This book is dedicated to the ancient and modern seers of the Vedas, astronomy, astrology and Vastu (the Indian science of space and architecture). My special dedication and thanks go to Professor Dharmanand Sharma, one of the finest modern day indologists

About this book

Many think that astrology is for predicting future and they can have a better hold on their lives if they know about the happenings beforehand. This is an erroneous notion, as in the Vedic tradition and culture, astrology is not meant to predict future, as nobody can predict future entirely. If everything was predetermined, then where is the human freedom? Astrology predicts principally the results of our past karma and the only way to counteract the results of the past karma is through present karma. Therefore, astrology is meant to direct you and to help develop your positive qualities and provide you guidance for eradicating the factors or qualities that lead you ultimately to bad fortune.

This book is meant to teach you simple numerological methods that you can beneficially use in your everyday life. You will find facts about your personality, how to modify your negative characteristics and how to enhance your positive characteristics. A quality can be used for both, destructive and constructive purpose and you will learn how to divert your energies for beneficial purpose.

This book teaches you to calculate the disturbed periods in your life and do your best to go through them calmly and peacefully.

How to use this book?

Study this book in a systematic manner in order to get maximum benefit from this wisdom based on the most ancient living traditions of the world. Learn step by step in the following manner.

❖ First of all, learn to calculate your life number and other important numbers related to you with the methods given in the first Chapter.

❖ In the second Chapter, learn about the importance and qualities of the individual numbers. Try to understand the philosophical basis behind each number and their importance in your life in relations to your life number. Learn about your personality traits.

❖ After you have gained enough experience in the above-said methods, learn to correlate different numbers related to your life number for making a horoscope.

❖ Learn to calculate the diverse life periods from the sum of age related to the life number and get over-difficult and disturbed periods of life with concentration practices and meditation on the symbolic significance of the numbers.

❖ Find your lucky numbers based upon your horoscope and use that knowledge to take decisions at the right time and place.

Contents

Dedication   5
About this Book   7
Introduction   11

Chapter 1   17
Your Numbers

Chapter 2   27
Numbers in the Vedic Tradition
and in your Life

Chapter 3   105
Making your Horoscope

Chapter 4   117
Periods of Change and Turmoil

Chapter 5   125
Your Lucky Numbers

Conclusion   131

About the author   *135*

Introduction

**Kriyabhedaye kalastu,
Sankhya sarvasya Bhedikam.**

The above Vedic citation means that diverse actions are based upon time or kala and kala is based upon numbers. To understand this, we must understand certain Vedic concepts. According to the holistic view of the Vedas, the universe is an indivisible whole and should be seen in its entirety. The whole cosmos functions on same principles and there is a fundamental unity in all what exists. However, to obtain knowledge about the universe, we have to divide it into smaller parts. That is where the importance of numbers lies. It is written in the scriptures: **Sankhyam bhavati gyanam.** This means that the numbers are related to knowledge. An individual is a part of the whole as a miniature cosmos in the vast cosmos and both are interrelated, interconnected and interdependent. However, when we talk about individual identity and the knowledge about it, we have to depend upon numbers.

The book is based on the Vedic tradition where the knowledge is said to depend upon numbers or analysis of the universe is done in terms of numbers. Significance of numbers for the present book is inspired from cosmogony and cosmology. Like the cosmos has its influence on us, these numbers also influence our day-to-day lives. Besides that, numbers play an important role in the living tradition of India for performing rituals and ceremonies. Performance of fire ceremonies, weddings, entrance into a new house (grihpravesh), naming the newborn, beginning a new work or business or starting a construction, and thousands of other daily rituals are performed on a calculated specific time and day. Since weddings are generally very elaborate, and they take place only at certain specific times of the year, wedding periods are chaotic in the big cities and create a problem of traffic.

Vedic mathematics is famous in the world and it gave humankind the concept of zero and decimal. In the Vedic tradition, the advanced astronomy and astrology and interaction of all what exists in the cosmos with each other is used to calculate the special dates for performance of the rituals and ceremonies.

The rosary used for japa (repetition of a mantra to get a thought-free mind) in yoga has 108 beads. The distance from the earth to the sun is 108 times the diameter of the sun. Thus, this number is used to reach the celestial plane. The sum of 108 is number 9 and this number is a complete number.

The present book demonstrates various concepts of the ancient Vedic wisdom related to the numbers and how they can guide you in your everyday life. Astrology is not for predicting future. Nobody can predict the exact future. Events and happenings in our life are the results of our karma. There are karma of the past life that decide the situation and circumstances of our birth and there are karma of this life. For our present karma, we use our sense of discretion or *buddhi*. The present karma is called *purusharth* in Sanskrit. In Ayurvedic terminology, the past and the present karma are distinguished as *daiva* and *purushkara*. Astrology can tell the results of our past karma and good and bad periods of life but nobody can predict our present karma and how we will act in a particular situation in future. Since the actual happenings in our life also depend as much on our present karma as on our past karma, therefore no astrological methods or the persons with clairvoyance can predict your future exactly.

Our characteristics related to the date of birth are the results of our previous karma. The number of our name relates to our present karma and our relationship with our parents and siblings or others who are closely associated with us during childhood. Our aptitudes, tendencies, interests, talents, gifts, dumbness, craziness, confusion or clarity or other allied traits which we seem to have from the beginning are due to the results of our previous karma. The sum total of the results of the previous karma is termed as sanskara. In a way, sanskara is the subtle memory over an extended period of time which is more than one life. With our present karma or purusharth; or in other words, with our efforts and persistence, we can make the best out of what we have brought with us from our past. Attaining the knowledge of the past karma is one way to accept it and it helps us to plan the present and the future better. It also provides us the fundamental wisdom of life and saves us from frustration or conceit that originates by comparing ourselves with others.

We human beings possess mind and power of discretion or buddhi, and with that we can ward off the negative results of our past karma. This can happen through japa (repetition of a mantra) and other concentration practices and doing good karma by doing selfless deeds, by helping other human beings, and by protecting and saving destruction of nature.

If we use astrology to guide us and show us the way of orienting our present karma in the light of our past karma, we can obtain fruitful results. Thus, this book on numerology is not meant only to teach you to find out about yourself and about your life events but it also provides you the wisdom to get rid of the unpleasant and enhance the agreeable and peaceful dimensions of life by coordinating your inner energy with the cosmic energy.

This book is not based on the Vedic Astrological system which is very exact and exhaustive and based upon the time and position of the planets. In this system, besides the date of birth, one needs to know the exact time of birth and the geographical location of the birth. The source of this book is the numbers in Vedic cosmogony and cosmology, which were later translated into rituals and ceremonies of the living tradition of present day India.

The most ancient school of thought from Ancient India is Samkhya that describes the reality of the cosmos in 25 components. The word Samkhya itself means numbers. Samkhya forms the fundamental basis of both yoga and Ayurveda. The concepts of Samkhya were later romanticized in the Puranas and other aspects of the tradition after the Vedic period. Besides that, it is my experience of nearly three decades of making numerological horoscopes that stands testimony to my methods of numerology used in this book.

Since for all practical purposes in the whole world, we use the Western Calendar that began with Christian era, I have also used this calendar for convenience. Besides that, the name alphabets are used in Latin to calculate the number of the first name.

It is simple to work with numbers and coordinate the important numbers of your horoscope with your day-to-day life for taking important decision and for important events in your life. The book is designed in such a way that you begin simply and with fewer numbers and learn and experience their significance in your life. After having acquired the fundamental wisdom of the basic numbers related to your life, you learn about the complicated calculations related to different periods of life.

For the best use of book, I suggest that you read the first and second chapters in order to find out your numbers and the importance of numbers in the cosmos.

Astrology is not only to depict and tell you about good and bad periods of life, but to guide you to take advantage of the good period and be cautious during bad period. With some spiritual practices, you can create sattva energy (inner stillness) and find a best way to deal with the results of your past karma as well as do the present karma for attaining health, peace, success and prosperity.

CHAPTER 1
YOUR NUMBERS

The reality of the cosmos for each individual begins from his or her own reality. We human beings represent the entire cosmos in a miniature form (Shudra Brahman). Therefore let us begin the game of numbers from you. Who are you in terms of numbers? There are following diverse numbers you will learn to calculate for yourself:

1. Your life number which is the sum of your date of birth.
2. The number of your first name.
3. The sums of your day, month and year of the birth individually.

Your life number

Total numbers are from one to nine. Each number has its own characteristics that you will learn in the next Chapter. Learn to calculate your life number from your date of birth and once you have calculated your number, perhaps you will be very curious to find its significance immediately. You can look up in the next chapter the different dimensions for your life number and the personality traits and characteristic– both negative and positive. However, for a total numerological horoscope, you will have to learn also to calculate the other above-mentioned numbers.

Example 1

First step:

Date of birth: 19-8-1998:   1+9+8+1+9+9+8= 45

Second step:

4+5= 9

Thus, the life number of the person born on 19th August 1998 is 9.

Example 2

10-1-2000:   1+1+2= 5

The life number of the person born on 10th January 2000 is 5.

Example 3

11-3-1935:   1+1+3+1+9+3+5= 23

2+3= 5

The life number of a person born on March 11th 1935 is 5

You have learnt to calculate the life number from your date of birth. Now I will give you examples of each number from one to nine.

Number 1:
23-9-1949:   2+3+9+1+9+4+9= 37   3+7= 10
10 is considered as number 1
1-3-1923:   1+3+1+9+2+3= 19   1+9= 10

Number 2:
2-4-1913:   2+4+1+9+1+3= 20   20 is considered as number 2
13-12-1930   1+3+1+2+1+9+3= 20

Number 3:
5-9-1960:   5+9+1+9+6= 30   30 is considered as 3
9-1-2000:   9+1+2= 12= 3

Number 4:
1-1-1901:   1+1+1+9+1= 13   1+3= 4
5-9-1961:   5+9+1+9+6+1= 31   3+1= 4

Number 5:
5-3-1968:   5+3+1+9+6+8=32   3+2= 5
2-1-2000:   2+1+2= 5

Number 6:
23-12-1951: 2+3+1+2+1+9+5+1= 24   2+4= 6

9-3-2001:   9+3+2+1= 15   1+5= 6

Number 7:
14-10-1900:   1+4+1+1+9= 16   1+6= 7
31-4-1952   3+1+4+1+9+5+2= 25   2+5= 7

Number 8:
16-2-1943:   1+6+2+1+9+4+3= 26   2+6= 8
29-11-1966   2+9+1+1+1+9+6+6= 35   3+5= 8

Number 9:
31-11-1902:   3+1+1+1+1+9+2= 18   1+8= 9
19-6-1982:   1+9+6+1+9+8+2= 36   3+6= 9

In addition to the one to nine numbers, there are double numbers which are not added. They represent the single number with double emphasis. They are 11, 22 and 33 and 44. It is not possible to get 55 or more. The maximum I get until now is 46 for the children born on 9-9-1999. Eight thousand years later, children born on 9-9-9999 will have number 54. Thus, nobody will get number 55 and therefore I mention the double numbers only up to 44.

Examples:

3-6-2000:   3+6+2=11
28-9-1936:   2+8+9+1+9+3+6= 38   3+8=11

12-6-1921:   1+2+6+1+9+2+1= 22
17-9-2003:   1+7+9+2+3= 22

4-9-1955:   4+9+1+9+5+5= 33
9-9-1950:   9+9+1+9+5=33

8-8-1999:   8+8+1+9+9+9= 44
19-9-1978:   1+9+9+1+9+9+7+8= 44

Importance of the life number

Life number is the principal factor to determine your fundamental personality. But every other number is also important and each number is viewed in relation to the life number. Remember that each number is important in its own way and it is not that persons of certain numbers are better or worse than others. The importance lies in knowing better about our fundamental resources and channelling them for creativity and efficiency.

Two persons of the same number may seem very different from each other due to how their energy is diverted. For example, if a number signifies will-power, it may be used in two diverse directions. It can be beneficially used to achieve an aim in life and can be also used for being stubborn and unnecessarily dominant. Second reason of diversity can be the presence of other numbers in the date of birth which can play a balancing role for the life number. The number of the first name is another factor that influences the life number.

The number of your first name

It is easy to calculate the number of your first name written in Latin alphabet. A letter represents simply the number it is occupying in the sequence of placement in the alphabetic table.

A = 1
B = 2
C = 3
D = 4
E = 5
F = 6
G = 7
H = 8
I = 9
J = 10 = 1
K = 11 = 2
L = 12 = 3
M= 13 = 4
N = 14 = 5
O = 15 = 6
P = 16 = 7
Q = 17 = 8
R = 18 = 9
S = 19 = 1
T = 20 = 2

U = 21 = 3
V = 22 = 4
W = 23 = 5
X = 24 = 6
Y = 25 = 7
Z = 26 = 8

For convenience, let us put the alphabetic numeral in another manner.

A, J and S are	1
B, K and T are	2
C, L and U are	3
D, M and V are	4
E, N and W are	5
F, O and X are	6
G, P and Y are	7
H, Q and Z are	8
I and R are	9

Examples of number calculation from your first name:

ISABELLE
9+1+1+2+5+3+3+5= 29 = 11

HORST
8+6+9+1+2 = 26 = 8

RADHA
9+1+4+8+1 = 23 = 5

SHYAM
1+8+7+1+4 = 21 = 3

MARIA
4+1+9+9+1 = 24 = 6

JOHN
1+6+8+5= 20 = 2

SUSAN
1+3+1+1+5 = 11

PAUL
7+1+3+3= 14 = 5

LUCILE
3+3+3+9+3+5= 26 = 8

TOMOE
2+6+4+6+5= 25 = 7

BRIGITTE
2+9+9+7+9+2+2+5=45 = 9

VANAJA
4+1+5+1+1+1 = 4

LINDA
3+9+5+4+1 = 22

You see that it is easy to calculate the number of your name in the above-described manner. Now we go to the next step to calculate the three numbers from day, month and year of your birth.

The individual numbers of your day, month and year of the birth

After having learnt the above calculations, you will find it easy to do these three simple calculations. Here are some examples:

Date of birth:
26- 8- 1951
8: 8: 7

Thus, a person born on August 26, 1951, has influence of numbers 8 and 7 besides the life number which is 5 in this case. The number 5 however remains the principal number, whereas the other numbers will define the attributes of this person. If this person's name is Paul, the influence of number 5 is very strong in his case.

Date of birth:
13- 11- 2001
4: 2: 3

This person was born on November 13, 2001, and numbers 4, 2 and 3 influence him/her besides the life number 9.
Date of birth:
11-10-1942
2: 1: 7

This individual with life number 1 has influence also of numbers 2, 1 and 7. This person has influence of number1 very strong, as it repeats several times and is also the life number. This person will have many folds the characteristic qualities of number 1.

Date of birth:
2-2-2002
2: 2: 4

This person's life number is 8 but number 2 has a tremendous influence on her/his life. This person has strongly the characteristic qualities of number 2.

Each individual number in the date of birth is important besides the calculations you have learnt up till now. But I will deal with all these later. First have fun with making your initial horoscope by relating your numbers to the significance of these numbers given in the next chapter.

Chapter 2

Numbers in the Vedic tradition and in your life

As stated earlier in the book, the numbers are one to nine. But before we begin the description of each individual number in the context of Vedic tradition, we must know the importance of zero or shunya. In our day to day life and in terms of value of things, zero alone has no value. Zero behind other numbers has value in multiples of ten, hundreds, thousands, and so on. In the Vedic tradition, the zero represents nothingness or void. Everything comes from shunya and dissolves back into shunya. Shivalinga is the symbolic representation of shunya that depicts the beginning and the end of the phenomenal world (see page 2 for Shivalinga).

The number One

Cosmos and gods

The ultimate reality is 'one' in the Vedic tradition. It is Brahman or the Universal Soul that is the cause of life. It is also called Purusha in Samkhya and Yoga. Brahman or Purusha is the living element of all that exists. It is the cause of life and its vitality. Although Brahman is the cause of life but alone it cannot make life and existence possible. It puts life into the Cosmic Substance called Prakriti. Purusha has no material; it is only energy. The energy can react through a substance and that is how the combination of Purusha and Prakriti make life possible.

Number one has uniqueness about it. Its strength is visualised in different cosmic bodies. The sun is the cosmic representation of number one. Radiant, unique and full of energy, the sun dominates the cosmos and the phenomenal world. It is the symbol for radiance, beauty and fame.

Ganesha is mostly shown alone and is worshipped before all the other gods. He is a child god and is worshipped for a good beginning and success in a project.

Born out of wind, the god Hanuman is a loan god. He symbolises strength and movement and is the conqueror of space. He is worshipped for courage, strength and victory.

The goddess Kali— the goddess of time is also alone. Time destroys everything and the new things are born out of this destruction.
God Vishvakarma is the creator god and he is always alone.

Ceremonial and ritualistic tradition

According to the Vedic tradition, there are ten directions of the cosmos. The four major directions make four angles and that makes eight directions. The additional two directions are upper and lower representing space and earth. This concept is used in all the traditional ceremonies for paying homage and for giving offerings. Construction of a pyramid is based upon these ten directions.

Amongst five elements that constitute all what exists in the phenomenal world, the first element is aakasha or space. Without space, nothing can exists. The other four elements exist in space. Thus, the significance of number one is also vastness.

In the Hindu moon calendar, the first day of the new moon is considered holy and is called Ekadashi.

Persons of Life Number One

Number 1 is a unique and powerful number with the qualities of ruling, dominating and leadership. Brahman symbolising number one and is the cause of life. But remember that despite its power of life, Brahman alone is not life. Life begins only when Brahman comes in contact with the Prakriti, the Cosmic Substance. Thus, despite being strong, powerful and dominating, people with life number one have their dependability on others and have a soft side of personality. They never like to accept their loneliness and always keep a brave façade.

Individual with life number one can be compared with a coconut which is very soft inside despite its hard cover. The nut inside the hard cover has numerous medicinal qualities and is delicious. But to reach the soft and delicious nut, one needs to break the hard cover with patience and skill. Similarly, number one individuals have generally an enriched personality despite being formidable.

The individuals of number one are usually dynamic and they do not give up very easily. They can charm you with their radiance but you may be disappointed if you come to know them a little more because of their dominating character.

The number ones are direct, straightforward and determined. They do not like hypocrisy and rather sometimes they are so straight forward that their family and friends feel uncomfortable with them. Some of the number ones are blamed for 'lacking culture' because of their excessive straight forwardness. This however depends if there are other number ones in their horoscope besides the life number, which provides an individual extreme characteristics of this number.

Because of their dominating character and leadership qualities, persons of life number one like to be professionally independent. When they are in job, they have always trouble with hierarchy and tend to fight with their bosses, which may prove destructive in some cases. Those of you who have other heavy numbers like 8 or 9 in the horoscope usually end up with a successful independent profession.

Number one persons are generally very ambitious as they want to prove themselves to be unique. For that, they make lot of effort rightly or wrongly. They get depressed or feel uncomfortable with themselves if they are unable to achieve according to their plans. But that lasts only for a short while as their determination drives them to make an effort afresh.

These persons are generally multidimensional and they are successfully capable of changing their profession or in bringing in multiplicity in their domain of work. This is because the number one signifies vastness. Individual with this life number are hard working. As they are ambitious and want to be well known and recognised, and they work for it. They are well directed in life and are usually self-confident.

The number one persons seek attention from others and do not like to be ignored or left alone in a group. They are quite independent in their work but they want recognition of their achievements. If they do not get attention from the family or society, they attract attention by talking about their achievements. In other words, they are not very humble. I do not mean to say that all number ones are creative and achieve something. Just the simple and modest persons may want attention of others to admire their house, their family and success of their children.

Number one in the family

They are a guide and a mentor to their children and to all others who desire to learn from them. Their companion finds them rather dominating and the trouble begins if their companion is also number 1.

These individuals are dominating in the family as well, and their families are happier if these persons have jobs or work which satisfies their leadership qualities. For example, number one as parent are better parents if they are bosses outside their home. A number one mother who is a housewife tends to dominate in the family. It will do the family good if she starts doing some social work or participate in other activities outside the house. Similarly, a number one father or husband may disturb the familial harmony after their retirement. It is better for the family if they remain busy with other activities after retirement.

The number one children are very good in the family if they are doing well in their education. They usually want recognition from their parents for their success at school or in sports or other extracurricular activities. But if they are not good at school, they give trouble to parents and siblings in wanting to have their own way in everything. They do that until they have found their aim in life. Once they have a goal, be it gardening or collecting strange things or travelling, they leave others in the family at peace and get involved in achieving their aim.

Health of number one

The persons with life number one are generally born with good health but due to their present karma, they may ruin their health and become prey to the ailments. What I mean is that sometimes they insist so much on achieving their aim that they ruin their health. Since they have a strong will power and strong sense of direction, they ignore every other thing. For some individuals of number one, their physical appearance and health becomes very important as they want to attract attention and want to shine like the sun wherever they go. These ones maintain their health and keep well as health is one of their aims.

The number one individuals should take care of their eyes (vision), skin and hair. They should not work at the cost of their health.

Companions and friends of number one

Individuals of number 5, 6 and 7 are good companions and friend for number one individuals. In fact the seven are the best. Numbers one and two together become the cause of friction and the companionship and friendship does not last very long. The other numbers (3, 4, 8 and 9) usually benefit from the sense of direction and strong will power of number 1. They also bring to number one their abilities and talents but are less tolerant to number one as compared to numbers 5 and 7.

Care suggestions and advices to number One

The persons of this number are at their best when they are teachers, leaders or consultants. They need to canalise this dominant energy in them otherwise they become troublesome in their relationship. They make good consultants or do well in jobs concerning sale, as they are good at convincing others with their strong character. If their profession is such that they are not the bosses and they have problems with those higher in hierarchy than them, they should canalise their energy in teaching their skills to others or become group leaders for a hobby or start something new with friends and inspire them for something different like going trekking in the mountains or some other likewise adventure.

The individuals of number one should pray to the sun for guidance and showing them way. They should pray to the sun for protecting them and taking right action in face of problems as these individual often get trouble related to their profession, if not then related to their family and friends.

The Number Eleven

The number eleven is not considered as two but an intense number one. It means, all the qualities described above are in a great intensity in a person of number eleven. The individuals with double number have sometimes extreme qualities which can be diverted in both negative and positive way. If you are number eleven, please read the description above and think that the characteristics described above are present with greater force in you than stated above.

The Number Two

Cosmos and gods

When the two energies come together, the cosmic drama begins. It is with the union of Purusha and Prakriti that the phenomenal world begins and all actions or karma begin. The cause of being, the Purusha, puts life into the lifeless Cosmic Substance, the Prakriti. Our being has also that duality of the substance we are made of (five elements) and the invisible energy of soul that enlivens the body and makes the mind and intellect function.

The combination of Purusha and Prakriti gives rise to three major elements for the beginning of the cosmos. These three elements make the reality of the cosmos made of twenty components. Thus, once again, number two is very important in the cosmic table and is symbolic of happenings and movements.

Moon is the symbol of number two. Moon is split into two phases. Moon is never the same for two consequent days. Unlike the hot and dynamic sun, the moon is cool and its radiations are tender. Moon is the symbol of mysticism and wisdom.

Gods with their companions are symbolic of number two. The yogi Shiva had a very eventful life with his consort Parvati through many lives in different forms. Krishna with Radha symbolise the eternal love and there were numerous ups and downs during the short time they were together. The wonderful form of Ardha-narishvara of shiva and Parvati symbolises the fusion of two into one. That means, it is a symbol of both one and two but two in complete harmony with each other in a state of fusion. Ganesha with Lakshmi is worshipped for a good beginning for material gains.

The second of the five elements that constitute the cosmos is air. Air is present in space. Air is always in momentum and its quality is to circulate. It is a quality that is opposite to the stability of the earth, which is the fifth fundamental element constituting the cosmos.

Ceremonial and ritualistic tradition

The number two is important for ceremonies and rituals. For the Yjanas, (the Vedic fire ceremonies, the couple sits together for the performance and similarly for the wedding ceremonies, the presence of both the parents of the girl is essential. After wedding, the couple symbolises oneness of the two. This is the submergence of the male-female energies. The male-female union results in the propagation of our cosmos.

Persons of Life number two

The number two is for events and happenings. Thus, these individuals generally have an eventful life. It is rare that the persons with life number two have a very straight and simple life as defined by the particular norms of their society. They have either some happening with their parents like separation or divorce or losing one parent at a very young age or their own relationships are troublesome. Some of the number two individuals have unusual childhood with their grandparents or in a hostel far away from home with lot of happenings.

Happenings can be positive or negative. In reality, they are the combination of both, as also from the negative and painful experiences, we imbibe lot of wisdom. So is the case of number two individuals. They learn a lot through their experiences. Many of the number two individuals are wise but they may not be able to give a practical shape to their wise ideas. Many a times, the synthesis and appropriate expression of their knowledge is lacking because of their ever changing nature. In other words, there is a lack of stability in these individual. In fact nothing is stable in this dynamic cosmos and this itself is the fundamental wisdom to understand the world.

Unlike persons of life number one, the persons of number two are not unidirectional and working towards one goal. They are split and indecisive at times. It is quite possible for them to be split between two professions and some of them leave their studies half-way to opt for something else which is quite different. They enjoy the diversity of life and want to experience different things. They have lot of experience than the others but the negative part of this wealth of experience is that they become indecisive.

There are individuals of number two who have great capability to integrate the diverse sort of wisdom. These ones are very successful in the fusion of wisdoms, ideas or scientific facts and make great discoveries. Think of the Ardhanarishvara- the fusion of male and female energies in Shiva. When the diversity is fused with each other, the two energies come in complete harmony and there is state of bliss or ananda. Thus, some number twos with harmony have great interest and capabilities for mysticism. In general, strange and mysterious things do happen with persons of life number two. I do not mean to say anything with ghosts or evil spirits. These are just unusual experiences with meeting different people or some events which do not occur so often. These events may have an exciting effect, they may bring something positive or at other times negative. Thus, there is diversity in these experiences. This quality should not be taken in the negative sense.

Because of their diversity, the individuals of number two may be hard to understand for others. Usually, they are humble and do every effort to make others understand them. They explain a lot about themselves and about the things in general. They love to narrate but their narration may be confusing at times. They tend to grumble about the happenings and people in their life. This happens especially if the number of their name or of day, month or year is also two.

The individuals of life number two are sweet natured and are flexible. They are easy to convince. They are not tough persons like those of life number one. But they confuse others with their dilemma. On the contrary, some of them are versatile and not confused. Some may go through these phases.

Lack of courage is another personality trait of number two individuals. It is also related to the trait of their being indecisive. However, with little spiritual guidance, this problem is solved.

Number two in the family

They bring always new things in the family and are full of diverse ideas. With the children of number two, the mother has to clarify twice each time about the wish of her child. Kids of number two tend to speak such a language that it is not clear whether they want an egg or a toast or both. This is due to the fact that they themselves are not clear. The parents of number two are very indulgent with their children. Children enjoy these parents as they are easy to convince. Clever children with life number one and nine take advantage of this fact and try to have their own way. The children of life number one always have an upper hand on their parents with number two due to their strong will. Number nine children also tend to have their way with number two parent due to their skill in argumentation.

Health of number two

These individuals are very sensitive and have more mental than physical problems. Because of the diversity of number two, they go through many paradoxical experiences and some of them suffer due to that. The indecisiveness of number two troubles many of them and gives them mental pain. They wish to depend on others for some decisions. That can cause both mental and physical problems. Other than this, they are sensitive in their chest region and should take care by doing regular pranayama. They should also take care with frequent cough and cold and treat immediately their sinus blockades if any.

Companions and friends of number two

If both the partners are number two, there is a mess. Number one and two are too diverse to be in harmony with each other. The individuals of number two are best in their partnership and friendship with four and eight. The earthy energy of the persons with four life number and organisational skills of number eight are very beneficial for number two individuals. They can also get along well with number five and seven.

Care, suggestions and advices to number two

The individuals of number two should use positively their ability of duality. For example, they should pursue a hobby or do a side-business or something alike to canalise their natural capabilities positively. The hobby or another sub-profession they should pursue should be very different from their principal profession.

The persons of number two should pray to the moon for their inner peace. Their peace is disturbed generally due to two reasons— when they are unable to take a decision and go through mental struggle for that or when they grumble. With their grumbling, they can make others unhappy around them. They should train their minds that they should divert all their mental energy to concentrate on moon whenever they are internally disturbed due to these two factors.

The Number Twenty-two

As described for number eleven, the number twenty two is the intense number of the number two. It is not considered as number four but has all the qualities of number two in great intensity. All the description above is applicable to this number but you should always think that the intensity of events and happenings is much more here.

The number three

Cosmos and gods

Number three in cosmic table of Samkhya is for creativity. When Purusha and Prakriti come together, the life begins. Their coming together gives rise to the sense of discretion, the ego and the Cosmic Mind. From these three originate the rest of the twenty-two elements that form the cosmic reality.

Prakriti or the Cosmic Substance has three fundamental characteristic qualities or triguna called sattva, rajas and tamas. Sattva is stillness and peace, rajas is action and tamas is that quality which stops action. All these qualities are in perfect balance in Prakriti but after Purusha brings life and the phenomenal world begins, the three qualities constantly change due to karma. Thus, in cosmos, the number three is associated with action and creativity. From the point of view of Ayurveda, the ancient Indian science of life and healing, we human beings have the three principal energies or tridosha which are responsible for all our mental and physical functions. They are called vata, pitta and kapha. Thus, again at physiological level, the number three is involved with action and formation. At the mental level, the three above-described gunas are the three modifications of the mind.

The third element of the fundamental elements that constitute the phenomenal world is fire. Fire can exist only with the presence of space and air. Significance of fire is energy and dynamic.

The creation, maintenance and destruction symbolise the cosmic cycle. The trinity of gods-Brahma the creator, Vishnu, the maintainer and Shiva the destructor maintain the cosmic balance. Shiva's destruction symbolises that Purusha and Prakriti come apart from each other and the phenomenal world comes to an end. Creation happens again, when they come together and the phenomenal world as a system is symbolised by Vishnu.

At another level, the trinity of Shiva, Parvati and their child Ganesha symbolise the perfection and harmony. This symbolises the creation at worldly level. That means having progeny, building a house and creativity at the level of material gains.

Ganesha with goddess Lakshmi and Sarasvati form another important trinity amongst the Hindu gods. Lakshmi is the goddess of material gains and dexterity whereas Sarasvati is the goddess of wisdom. These three signify together i) beginning a projects with a good aim and for sattvic cause (Ganesha), ii) with hard work and perseverance (Lakshmi that represents rajas energy) and doing work with wisdom by using one's sense of discretion, buddhi (Sarasvati that represents the sattva energy).

Shiva, Parvati and Ganesh in the form of trinity are worshipped for the familial well being, People hang their picture in their homes and business places for material gains, as well as to develop their abilities and capabilities for a harmonious life.

The three goddesses form another important trinity and they represent the three qualities of Prakriti or the Cosmic Substance. They also signify three dimensions of feminine energy. Sarasvati, Lakshmi and Kali represent sattva, rajas and tamas. These three represent respectively the creative energy, the energy of the action and energy of destruction that ends all actions. Women have more sattva and tamas energy in them as compared to men who have more rajas energy in them (refer to my book- *The Kamasutra for Women*).

Ceremonial and ritualistic tradition

Tri is Sanskrit is three and used as a prefix to describe number three. Tri is of great importance in ceremonial, ritualistic as well as medical and scholarly tradition of India. Here are some examples of the importance of three:

Tridosha: the body's three vital energies— vata, pitta and kapha.

Triguna: the three fundamental qualities of the cosmos and three different modifications of the mind.

Trishul: Shiva's trident symbolising triguna of the cosmos.

Triphala and trikuta: These are two Ayurvedic basic drugs each containing three substances. These two combinations are used for making different drugs along with other substances.

Tirveni: It is the pilgrimage at Allahabad where three rivers combine with each other— Ganga, Yamuna and hidden Sarasvati. This place is also called Prayag. Prayag holds the biggest festival of the world called Kumbha Mela every twelve years.

Trisathali: The three famous pilgrimage done together— Prayag, Kashi (Varanasi) and Gaya (in Bihar).* It is said that these are the most important pilgrim centres and no Hindu pilgrimage is complete without visiting these centres.

Triambke: This is the synonym for the three-eyed goddess Durga and this name is repetitively chanted in the ceremonial mantras for the goddess.

---

* Near Gaya, the Budha was enlightened under a Peepal tree and this satellite town of Gaya is called Budha Gaya- a famous Buddhist pilgrim centre now.

Tripitak: The teachings of the Buddha are assembled in three bodies of literature called the Tripatak.

Trilok: In the Vedic tradition, there is a mention of three worlds— Akasha (sky), dharati (earth) and patala (inside the earth).

Trishanku: The literal meaning of the word is 'one who has done three major bad karma. Trishanku is a very amusing character in Mahabharata. He wanted to go to heaven with his human body. He tried to do that with the help of a rishi but Indira, the lord of heaven pushed him down. The rishi send him back to heaven. Finally, Trishanku remained hung upside down between earth and heaven.

Persons of life number three

The persons of life number three are recognised by their dynamic character and for their love for aesthetics and beauty. Many of them take up art in one form or the other. Some complain that they wanted to be a musician, or painter or sculptor, and so on but their parents dissuaded them. In many cases, their energy for creativity and beauty is canalised in decorating their houses or gardens or dressing up very aesthetically if they do not have profession or hobby in the art in one form or the other.

The individuals of this life number are generally patient and listen to you attentively, but are not easily convinced. They need time to think and if they need to convince you, they do that with patience.

The creative energy of some number three individuals is concentrated on purely worldly things like family, having children, bringing them up very nicely with beautiful clothes and building beautiful houses. They spend lot of time in decorating their homes, doing their interiors as well as making beautiful gardens. It does not however mean that the number three of this category are only rich people who can afford to spend money on these things. These individuals and their houses are spotted out even in the middle class and poor colonies. In my village in the Himalayan Mountains as well as in other villages of the area, many times I spot out an exclusive house with very simple things and made very attractive. The kitchens in these houses are also very well decorated with their traditional utensils and water pots. Some make clay sculptures and pots to decorate their houses.

There is another category of number three who have their entire fiery element in one art form and family and social life is no more important for them. In fact, these ones may look quite contrary to the above described individuals simply because their creative energy is concentrated on one goal.

The individuals of number three are usually intelligent along with being creative. But they are lacking in leadership qualities and tendency to go ahead in life. Many of them remain unaware of their talents and feel very happy on being appreciated.

The persons of this number can be quite unstable and some of them tend to be reckless. They are always looking for a change. In that process, sometimes they destroy too much. In any case, the individuals of this number have some self-destructive tendencies.

The number three persons always tend to ignore, disregard or reject a new idea. But they do not insist upon their opinion and just need time to think it over. They may come to you a little later and say, 'finally I think you are right'. Their triangular personality and energy let them see more than the others and very spontaneously they feel that there are other possibilities. But once they think it over, they are able to distinguish between the creative ideas and destructive ideas.

It is a part of their creative nature to go to adventurous tourism and to explore other rejected and unexplored themes. Sometimes these individuals can work like crazy on some small detail of any theme which is not important to the world in general. The individuals of number three do not care generally what the world thinks about them or their work. For example they may choose to take up a research project on a theme which is completely ignored and unexplored. Thus, some of them may choose rather a tough path for themselves. Depending on the other numbers in their horoscope, they either achieve great success or gradually destroy themselves. Some of them have repeated failure due to their crazy ideas and therefore they feel depressed and ultimately become bitter. Think of the three edges of a triangle. When in bad circumstances, number three use them as weapons for self-defence. Ultimately they lose all their friends, except the persons who are extremely indulgent with them.

Number three in the family

These persons bring lot of creativity into the family. As said above, the creative talent of number three is expressed very spontaneously in their home environment. Number three children show their artistic expression in one way or the other during their early childhood. Sometimes their talents are suppressed by their parents saying that they should study something more practical and career oriented. Number three mothers are very encouraging for the artistic talents of their children. In fact, many of them believe that all children have it spontaneously and are disappointed if their child does not paint or play music. Number three fathers are frustrated if their family members do not show interest in making their home aesthetic or maintaining them well.

Fiery element of the number three men can cause problems in companionship. They need an indulgent companion who can appreciate their other talents that compensate for their inconsistent behaviour.

Health of number three

The self-destructive tendencies of number three can cause ill health. For example, those ones who crazily get into the unexplored themes may do excesses like keeping awake late, drinking too much coffee or doing other deeds to harm themselves. Creativity is a great force within oneself and for expressing that, one needs energy. Individuals of this number should try to keep a balance and always make sure that they replenish their energy. Specifically, they should take care of their vision and digestive fire of the body called agni in Ayurveda. Other sensitive organs for threes are lungs and heart. Lungs, liver and heart are together make Hridya according to Ayurveda. Hridya is also a word for heart but in medical terminology, this word describes the above mentioned three organs as they are interdependent and malfunctioning of one of them leads to the malfunctioning of the others as well.

Companions and friends of number three

Number three are generally in harmony with life numbers 4, 5 and 9. Fours give them their earthy energy, fives give them their balance and nines give them their rationality to proceed ahead and also exposing their talent to the world. The companionship with the same life number can be successful provided they have same profession or creative interest and they work under same roof or in same organisation.

Care suggestions and advices to number three

The individuals of this number should try to consider also the practical aspects of life. They should think of turning some of their creative ideas into material gains so that life can be financially smooth. They should also make an effort to maintain a balance between their family and social life, and their professional and creative activities. They should learn to weigh the positive and negative clauses before abruptly deciding something. They should review their life's events and learn from the past events to stop their self-destructive tendencies.

The Number Thirty-three

As described for numbers eleven and twenty-two, this double number is not considered as six but as intense number three. The descriptions stated above apply also to this number but in greater strength. Since number three is already a number with intense qualities, number thirty-three individuals tend to be distinguished and are easily remarked with their intense creativity or simply a desire to become an artist along with a tendency of destruction. Please pay attention to the care and suggestions described above to create balance in your life.

The number four

Cosmos and gods

The importance of number four in the Vedic tradition is due to the four major Vedas, namely the Rig, Yajur, Sam and Atharva Veda. The fundamentals of the tradition that flourished on the Indian continent are from the wisdom of these Vedas.

There are four major directions in the cosmos. The rest of the six directions are based on the four major directions. The ten directions represent the cosmos whereas the four directions represent our practical life on planet earth. Thus, the number four is symbolic of practical and material life on this earth.

Although the fourth element constituting the phenomenal world is water, in numerology, this number is symbol of earth— water being a part of it. The earth is supposed to have all the other elements of the cosmos and is considered complete. Our planet earth has water on one-third of its surface. The number four is the symbol of balance and harmony.

Gods and goddesses are generally represented with four arms, thus representing power, might and efficiency.

The most common picture of the gods in four is that of lord Rama with his consort Sita, his younger brother Lakshaman along with god Hanuman. From the story of Ramayana, these four symbolise sacrifice, love, sincerity, righteousness, effort, devotion and victory. Shiva and Parvati are mostly shown with their sun Ganesha but they have two sons. The other one is Kartikey. Kartekey is the symbol of beauty. Thus, these four represent the cosmic family in its perfection.

Ceremonial and ritualistic tradition

The number four is an important number in ceremonies, rituals, architecture, sculptures and other art forms. Square is always drawn representing the cosmos during various rituals and ceremonies. In the square, various planets are symbolically represented and offering are made to each one of them during fire ceremonies (yajana), land worship, ceremony for a new house, weddings, and so on. In vastu, the Indian science of architecture, the square is equally important to determine the exact placement of various rooms, kitchen, water source, etc. in a house. In a given piece of land of any shape, a square is first made approximately in the centre to work out the directions.

Number four is very important in temple architecture. The east facing temple has four corners of its dome. Before entering the room where deity resides, we enter into three other rooms which are quadrangular in shape.

Fourth day of the waxing moon falling at the end of August or the beginning of September is the birthday of Ganesha, the god of wisdom, good fortune and prosperity. It is also the god to be worshipped in the beginning of all the ceremonies. His birthday is called Ganesh Chaturthi and is celebrated all over India with festivity.

Persons of life number four

Persons with this life number are practical and down to earth. The most fundamental aspects of life are of foremost importance for these individuals. One category of number four are those who love nature and they may get extremely involved with minerals, trees and do travels to faraway places to explore nature. They are devoted to their gardens. They love land and like to get farm houses. Some of them may leave cities to settle in the countryside. They take activities or professions where they can appreciate the splendour of nature. They generally like to spend their holidays exploring nature. Depending upon their other numbers, some of them may take up adventure hobbies like mountain climbing, rafting, sailing and exploring the least known parts of the world. There are also people in this category who like to collect stones, feather, butterflies, flowers, and so on.

There is another category of number four which value material things more than nature. They love jewellery, nice clothes and other apparel that make them exclusive and attractive. They lay a great importance to these material things. It is equally important for them to decorate their houses and they lay a great importance to their vehicles and extravagant lifestyle.

There is yet another group of number four which form a medium between the two above described categories. They have the characteristics of both the above-described types but in a milder way. For example, they like to dress well and lay importance to their general appearance but they are not over-involved with it. Similarly, they love nature and like to spend time wandering in the forests and hills but come back to their urban home.

Some of the number fours have the negative tendency of dwelling over their past. Even when they are seventy, they are talking about their childhood and narrate to you their sufferings. They do not like to look forward and somehow get stuck to their past. On one hand, they talk about their past sufferings; on the other hand, they do not like to change their former habits. They also dwell upon past by narrating to you about their past adventures and achievements. You cannot have a good discussion with some of the number 4, specially the one who have this number several times. They go back to their past events from time to time and appear extremely self-centred.

Number fours are generally patient people, especially the one whose energy is concentrated on nature. Many of them are generous and accommodating. They are sincere and like to keep in touch also with far away friends.

The persons of this number are generally accumulating kind. They collect all kinds of things, some with the hope of doing something 'later', and others because they just like them. Depending upon the presence of other numbers in their entire horoscope, some of the number fours have houses full of various goods. The number fours with materialistic orientation have more the accumulating urge than the others who have their bent of mind to associate with nature. But these ones may accumulate other kinds of things like seeds, specimen plants or just grow too many plants in a smaller area.

Number four in the family

Due to their earthy nature and patience, the number fours generally make good parents. However, some number fours are found too boring by their family due to their repetitive past stories and due to forcing their own outdated notions on their children. They do not persist but expect that their children should be as they themselves were in their childhood.

Number fours are generally true companions and sincere by nature. Number four mother sometimes can become too possessive and doing too much for her children to the extent that the children do not become independent. Number four children have stable nature and can very well be alone and play alone. Some number four children are not so communicative and may face difficulty during initial years of schooling.

Number four may have difficulty with other numbers in the family due to their accumulating habits. This happens more when people live in smaller surfaces and some family members want them to throw some of their accumulated goods. Others should convince them patiently and cleverly and not drastically.

Health of number four

There are two aspects of health of number fours. The ones who are extremely attached to nature keep healthy. They have generally profound understanding of life due to observing nature and are also fussy about eating good quality organic food. The other category of number four who are attached more to the material aspects of life have often health problems. Persons of such category are more devoted to sensuous aspects of life and find joy in satisfying their senses. In this process, they do excesses with eating all kinds of foods and many take to regular or excessive drinking.

Persons of this number tend to put on weight and some of them become very lethargic. They should avoid eating too many sweet tasting things. In the Vedic tradition, sweet does not mean simply products containing sugar. It also includes most grains, like wheat, rice, barley, etc., potatoes and similar products, milk and milk products. Thus, bread will be included in this category. Sweet is associated with heaviness and contains earth and water energy. Excess of this food can make people lethargic and passive.

Companions and friends of number four

The number fours who are devoted to nature get along very well with each other. However, the ones with more attraction for materialism of life and their own body need someone with more balance and stillness like number five or seven. The nature loving fours generally do not get along well with numbers one and nine. Nine are too rationalistic for them and they seek reason in everything. However the nature loving fours know that everything is constantly changing, life is unpredictable and variations, sudden changes, catastrophes are equally a part of life. Numbers one and nine are not patient and indulgent enough to listen to the long and often self-indulging narrations from those number fours who are materially oriented.

Numbers five and seven also make good companions for number four. Persons of number three with number four may make a chaotic relationship. Number six is fine but eight may find number four disturbing due to their accumulative nature. Eights are well organised individuals.

Care, suggestions and advices to number four

Both types of number fours should avoid extremes. One extreme of number four is immersed in nature and forget the self— like taking care of one's appearance, dressing properly, etc. They must realise that they are a part of nature and they need also to make themselves beautiful like nature. The other self-indulgent extreme of number four should make an effort to broaden their horizon by taking part in social activities and by doing social service for the sick and needy.

Some number four individuals tend to eat heavy and sweet foods that lead to lethargy, weight problems and depression. They should take care with their diet and eat lighter foods with various spices. Persons of number four should be careful with the formation of abscesses and tumours which generally result from bad food and lethargy. The ones with love for nature do not get this problem, but the other category which are city oriented should devote their energy to proper movements, right diet, yoga and pranayama (yogic breathing practices).

The number forty-four

Like for the previously described double numbers, forty-four is not eight but an intense number four. The characteristics described above are present in an intense form in this number. Double digit number has strong character as compared to the single digit and certain tendencies and hobbies become their passion. Please follow the care and suggestions described above.

The number five

Cosmos and gods

All what exists in the phenomenal world is made of five elements— ether, air, fire, water and earth. Although it is the combination of these elements that makes the existence possible, yet the five elements are not the cause of existence or consciousness. Concrete and material aspect of existence is formed by the five elements but the dynamism of cosmos comes from the Purusha— the Universal Soul. Nevertheless, it is the dynamism of the five elements which is the cause of all phenomena. For example, a tiny seed becomes a mighty tree with the passage of time with the combination of the five elements. In fact the time or kala is defined with the dynamism of the five elements. The tiny seed becomes a sprout in earth, turns around, sends the roots in the ground and stem in the air, feeds itself from the sun and the water and keeps growing. Thus, number five is dynamic and mysterious both.

The number five is also the central number and signifies balance and harmony. In Samkhya cosmic table, besides the five fundamental elements, there are five subtle elements, five sense organs and five organs of action. All these four units of five numbers coordinate within their own unit as well as with each other. Thus, the number five is the number of coordination, coherence and harmony.

In the Yoga darshana or the yoga school of thought, Patanjali has described five kinds of modifications of mind (vritti) and five kinds of afflictions of the mind (klesha).

According to Vedanata darshana (Vedanata School of thought), the human body is divided into five different layers called Panchakosha— the physical body, the organs of action along with consciousness, mind, buddhi and the soul. In the Yoga Sutra of Patanjali, there are five major pranayama practices called prana, samana, apana, udana and vyana. They signify sending the vital breaths to chest, navel, lower abdomen, head region and all over the body (see my book, 'Programming Your life with Ayurveda' for the practical applications of these practices in everyday life).

Ceremonial and ritualistic tradition

Number five is important in many traditional ceremonies, rituals, nutrition and medical preparations. Here are some examples:

Panchagavya from cow— milk, curd, ghee, urine and dung:

The combination of these five products from cow is used in many medications in Ayurveda, namely for treating epilepsy.

Pancha dhanaya- wheat, barley, rice, moong and sesame:

This is a combination of five different grains which is used in some ceremonies as offerings and it is energy and immunity promoting.

Pancha pallava or five kinds of leaves for yajana ceremonies are mango, jamun, katha, Biroja and bel. These five plants are also medicinal plants and the leaves are offered in fire ceremonies. They give rise to perfumed smoke which is also used for inhalation.

The number five is important in the living Indian tradition. There are five different Kashis like Varanasi. They are Uttarakashi, Guptakashi, Varanasi (Kashi), Dakishan Kashi, Tenkashi. They are all residence of Shiva. Similarly, there are Panch Kedara, the five famous temples of Shiva located at the sites where Shiva dropped his five different parts of his body— sex organs

(Kedarnath in Gharwal region of the Himalayas), navel (Madmaheshwar), arms (Tunganath), head (Rudarnath) and hair (Kalpeshwar).

Pancha Deva are the combination of five gods— Vishnu, Shiva, Ganesha, Surya (the sun) and Durga.

In medicine there are panchamrit, pancharishtha and many alike.

Persons of life number five

These individual are generally balanced persons. Presence of other number fives besides the life number drives them to spiritual path. Many of the number five persons divert from routine path of life and wish to do something different to make the world better. In some, the drive to bring a change is so strong that they end up changing their profession.

Diversion towards spirituality or seeking a guru for guiding them for this path may be one of features of number five. Depending upon the other supporting numbers, number five may make spirituality a profession like teaching yoga or meditation or such similar subject that guide one for inner peace and stillness.

Number five individuals love to analyse everything and go into the details of all events and happenings. They are not looking for rationality and logic of the events but for the psychology and symbolism behind the happenings. They are also looking for he karmic reasons for those happenings. At times, they may irritate their friends and family with this behaviour.

The number five individuals generally have a holistic approach to life. They split ideas, theories, and philosophies only for understanding them in the finer sense and to see the correlation of the individual events. Without being conscious of it and without having any clarity in their mind, basically number fives believe that everything is interconnected and interrelated in this universe. This is the fundamental Vedic thinking that finds its continuity in Buddhism, Jainism and other religious traditions of Asia. The number fives born in the West are sometimes confused and do not understand themselves that opposes the reductionist way of thinking prevalent in the West. When these individuals are exposed to the holistic way of thinking coming from the East or from the Middle Ages in Europe, they feel comfortable and experience as if they have found themselves.

Some number fives may follow a religion or a sect seriously from their childhood and may follow an authority or the given set of rules in a systematic and organised way. However, sooner or later in their lives, they do have inner revolt

67

and depending upon their other numbers and their present karmic conditions, they may get out of the organised religions or sects.

Some number fives wish to become gurus themselves and that is due to the influence of the other numbers which orient them towards business and authority.

The average number five are the simple family oriented individuals who look for peaceful life and inner stillness. Usually they do not impose their ideas on others but do like to advise them from time to time about the importance of peaceful life.

The number five individuals are generally warm hearted and loving. However, some of them like to be aloof and oriented towards finding many unanswered questions in the world. They are easily withdrawn to mysticism and tend to read the lives of the saints or the Middle Age stories of the healers and mystics.

Some number fives may lack self confidence because they might find themselves different from others. This happens specially if number fives are surrounded by individuals of number one, eight and nine and may begin to think that something is wrong with them. This ensues due to their tendency to seek for subtle and hidden energy within themselves and in the cosmos. The others may start finding them weird. Many of the number fives therefore feel delighted in the company of the yogis and mystiques and gradually discover that this aspect of life they are attracted to exists and is experienced when the sensuous stops. With this experience, these individuals undergo a transformation and emerge with a shining personality.

Many number fives have different experiences of the subtle power of nature in their childhood. This of course is suppressed due to formal education and the school system based upon Western ideology of reality being exclusively sensuous and material. However, this aspect of their being comes back in their late thirties or early forties.

Number five individual can be best described as those having unity in diversity and diversity in unity. Just like the five elements of the cosmos unify to perform the functions of the universe, similarly one should understand the unity in diversity of number five persons. They are very good in coordination and uniting people. Just as the five elements have very strong independent characteristics and powers of their own, similarly the number fives have the marked individual traits of their personality and also they like to analyse the diversity of situations and events and see their practical aspects.

Number five in the family

As parent, number five individuals like to guide their children and others in the family but not with dominance like the number one but with subtlety. They are generally loved but their tendency to see the subtle reasoning for everything may make their children irritated at times. On the other hand, they are loved in their family for the same reason. That is because their subtle ways help solve disputes and problems in the family. If their children come home from school with a sad face, the sensitive number fives immediately know and ask them. They are able to provide them support by analysing their problem and teach them to be subtle in looking at life's ups and downs.

Generally number five children do well in school but sometimes with a wrong orientation, they divert from studies and have a tendency towards mysterious things. They divert their attention to read mystery murders or other similar stories or even learn astrology rather than science and mathematics.

Health of number five

The number five individuals are generally conscious of their body in a holistic sense and take care of their health. But there are some who follow certain sects or groups and may ruin their health with special and unreasonable food habits and lifestyle. But the positive part of number five is that they do realise their mistake before it is too late and correct it.

Since number five individuals have the basic traits of harmony and unity, they fundamentally take care of themselves. These individuals make the best out of their given health situation and tend to take wise path for themselves.

Individuals of this number should be careful with their general health. They tend to feel unwell with small irritants. They should also be very careful about not taking foods with all kinds of preservatives. Food with chemical is bad for everybody but the persons of number five are more sensitive. Actually, the body's immediate reaction to poisons is a positive sign, as they do not accumulate on a long term basis.

Companions and friends of number five

The number fives are suited with most numbers for companionship except number nine. Please recall that the compatibility of the two individuals as friends or companions also depends upon the other numbers of each individual in their charts. The number nine persons are rational and they are a little remote from the search for mysticism. They may clash with number five.

Some number fives may also find number one over-powering and dominating. But basically, number one likes number five as they help them to bring balance in their life. The individuals of number five and six make good friends and companions. Number six individuals have an earthy character that provides balance to number five.

The two individuals of number five can also make good friends and companions. However, with both the parents of number five, kids may have difficulty due to the intensity of their search with subtle energy. Children of number nine may find it particularly difficult with both the parents of number five.

Care, suggestions and advices to number five

These individuals should always avoid extremes like following a groups or a sect. In whatever direction their bent of mind is, they should always make sure that they are well informed before they decide to follow certain ideology, sect or religion. This is particularly important for those who have also another number five besides their life number. Those number fives who get into the right path of genuine yogic practices like japa and ekagrata as described by the Yoga guru

Patanjali, they are on the right path and they feel in harmony with themselves. A regular practice of ekagrata can bring the number fives at right path. Concentration practices do good to everybody, but it is an essential and karmic need for the persons of number five. They also need lesser effort than the others to achieve a still state of mind.

The number six

Cosmos and gods

There are six different schools of thoughts from ancient India called Shatadarshan. These school follow the Vedic tradition but have different point of view to explain the reality of the cosmos. All these schools have a common aim: liberation from the cycle of life and death. Yoga is one of these six schools.

Shata-tiratha: These are six different kinds of karma that have the similar results like doing the pilgrimage. These are: I) to be devoted to our real self soul, which is a part of the ultimate reality— the Purusha or the Universal Soul, ii) devotion for the guru who enlightens us with wisdom, iii) devotion for your mother, iv) devotion for your father, v) devotion for your guests & vi) devotion for your male or female partner.

73

Shadanan is the name of one of the two Shiva's sons also known as Kartike. It means the one who has six heads. Kartike is the symbol of beauty and love.

In the Vedic tradition, mind is considered as sixth sense and superior than the other senses. It is the organiser and the controller of all the five senses. In English and perhaps in other European languages also, one uses the expression 'sixth sense' for intuitive quality of mind.

The triguna (three characteristic qualities of the mind) and tridosha (the three energies of the body) together form the six dimensions of the human beings. At a physical level, the organisation of the body is done by three dosha (vata, pitta and kapha) which are constituted of the five elements (ether, air, fire, water and earth). The three qualities of the mind are sattva, rajas and tamas.

Ceremonial and ritualistic tradition

Shatkarma: Six different kinds of karmic rituals are recommended for every day: I) bath, ii) Gayatri mantra, iii) Havana (fire ceremony with offerings), iv) prayers, v) devotion to the higher powers (like the sun, moon, water, etc.) and vi) hospitable and good to guests and outsiders.

Shata-tila-ekadahsi: This is observance on the first day of the new moon (ekadashi) during the month of Magha that falls on mid-January. This is called shata-tila (six-sesames) as on this day, six different things are done with sesames seeds. These are: i) bath with water mixed with sesames seeds, ii) rubbing the body with sesames paste (ubtan), iii) fire ceremony with sacrificial sesames seeds, iv) drinking water mixed with sesames seeds, v) eating sweet preparations made of sesames and vi) donating sesames seeds. It is a ritualistic observance marking the end of winter and end of eating food that generates too much heat in the body. Sesame is an example of such foods.

Persons of life number six

Person of number six are generally balanced and harmonious. They may seem little slow to react, but they are very careful in taking decisions and they are compulsive in thinking too much regarding various aspects of a particular situation or a problem. At times, they may irritate others by asking too many questions and want to understand everything from different dimensions and different angles. These individual tend to be stable and sincere in their relationships to others and for their business commitments. In relationships, they may be difficult at times, as they are not so easily able to enjoy the lighter aspects of life. It does not mean that they do not have sense of humour or do not laugh. They are intense and do not like to waste time uselessly. Because of that they are very good in their work and many of them have skills of doing fine work that requires patience.

Unlike number one, these are not the ones who will dominate in a gathering. Number six are usually good listeners and they need time to react to an idea or an offer. But in this process, they may miss opportunities at times.

Number six persons are generally multi-dimensional with several different talents. Due to this quality they are generally surrounded by people who ask them for help in one way or the other. These individuals have the capability to put various pieces of the problems together and help others. At another level, they can help other people with their dexterity and talent about different dimensions of day-to-day living.

Some number six individuals may lose their direction due to their multidimensional ability and remain confused about the choice of a specific field. Some of them may get several job offers due to the same reason and again they face a state of dilemma. This may also apply in other walks of life. Their confusion is particularly seen in selection of big things like property, jewellery, etc.

In today's world with a reductionist approach to life we live in the age of super specialities. Some of number six may find themselves misfit. On the other hand, in jobs where multiple abilities are required, these persons are demanded and are successful.

The principal problem of number six individuals is their dilemma. Imagine the old kind of balances for weighing things. They are extremely sensitive when you hold them from their holding rod or thread. The balancing rod moves even with the wind. It is the same situation with these persons. They are often wavering between two ideas or two persons or two things. The dilemma may also be between what their heart says and what their mind thinks. Usually, they listen to their heart.

You should look at number six split between two threes. It is interesting that this dilemma is a part of their karmic personality and they are not easily worked up by this. Basically, they are cool and forget about their dilemmas easily or sleep over them.

Number six in the family

As said above, number six persons have the quality of stability and sincerity. Due to that, they are loved in their families. They command respect from their children and their partners find them trustworthy. However, they are subjected to criticism due to their hair splitting ways of analysing everything. But due to their trust, stability and earthy element, their children feel free to criticize them.

Number six parents are loving and giving. The number six children are easy to bring up, as they are capable of remaining busy with themselves. They also accept easily their circumstances and what the fate brings them. Please remember that fate in the Vedic tradition is the results of the previous karma.

Health of number six

Persons of this number tend to take care of themselves. They usually take it as one of the multiple things they have to learn and do. However, if they fall ill, they create big fuss about it, as they usually would like to treat themselves. As it is the character of the people of this number, they like to try different types of therapies.

These persons tend to be fussy about the balance in life and therefore take care about the balance in their food habits also. This is generally the secret of the health of this number.

Companions and friends of number six

Individuals of number six make good companion with any of the numbers because of their patience and stability. They share a lot in common with number four of the category who are bent towards nature. Number six can be good companions for numbers one and three. They may help to stabilise individuals of these numbers due to their earthy and stable nature and prevent them from reacting impulsively. They are also tolerant for them and make them think before they decide. Though the number one individuals may get irritated with them and find them slow, but their patience wins their hearts soon. Number five individuals can make good companions for number six persons. They can theoretically guide them in many ways and number five can bring the spiritual aspect in companionship and friendship.

Individuals of this number have very intense relationship with number seven. In fact, the presence of number seven completes their life and makes them fulfilled.

Care suggestions and advices to number six

Number six individuals are multi dimensional and they should make an extra effort to utilise this character. This can leave some of them confused and indecisive. They should accept this quality as karmic and make benefits from it by doing their present karma right and according to what they basically are. As number six individual, you should self examine your abilities in a detached manner and ask yourself but you prefer the most. Instead of undergoing the indecisive state of mind, direct your energy to pranayama practices and concentration exercises. When the mind is thought-free, it reaches a yogic state of mind which is called sattvic state and the right decision come automatically.

If the persons of other numbers, especially number one are impatient with you, make them understand that you need time. Let them not make you nervous. Do not let others force their decisions on you. Do yogic practices and listen to your own heart.

The number seven

Cosmos and gods

Saptrishi or the seven sages are mentioned in the Vedas. From the later literature, it seems that this denotes for the cosmic organisation and different energies that emanate from the Cosmic Mind or manas. In Vedic Samhitas, their names are not given but in later literature of Brahmans and Upanishads, their names are given with slight variations.

Saptrishi in Vedic astronomy is the name for Big Dipper asterism or the Great Bear. They are important also in Vedic astrology in relation to the constellation of the other stars and planets.

In Rig-Veda, the seven rays of Surya (the Sun) are stated parallel to the Seven Worlds of the seven planets driven by seven horses.

Based in Samkhya, yoga and Ayurveda, I have interpreted human existence in seven dimensions. For number six, I have stated the three energies at the physical level and another three energies at the mental level. However, the cause of being is soul that breathes energy into this six dimensional being. Thus the existence is seven dimensional.

Ceremonial and ritualistic tradition

The ancient Vedic civilisation (Indus Valley) is also referred to as Sapta Sindhu civilisation. The main centre of this civilisation was spread around Sindhu (Indus) river and Sarasvati river which had flown parallel to the Sindhu and is now dried out. The other five rivers of the North West India are Jhelam, Chanab, Ravi, Vyas and Satluj.

Sapta Puri are the seven tiratha or the pilgrimage centres from ancient India and this tradition is followed until today. These are:, Haridwar, Mathura, Ayodhya, Varanasi (also called Benaras or Kashi), Kanchipuram, Ujjain (Avantipuram) and Dwarka .

Persons of life number seven

The persons of number seven are mostly good natured and are generally diverted towards education and learning. They try to be perfectionist. I do not mean to say that they are perfectionist, but their karmic connection drives them to that direction. These are the individuals who always make an effort to be good to others. Some of them can be extremely selfless and participate in social work for the good of society. However, these individuals are very critical of the evils of the society and their social work involves eradicating the evils and just not being good for the sake of it or simply to add a good karma in their account. For examples, these individuals will not be satisfied by paying to some poor kids for education. They will rather open a school in a remote area to benefit multiple people and for generations to come.

The individuals of this number have patience and tolerance. They also have an inherent sense of contentment. They do not see rapidly the wrongs of the others and always give space to others. Generally they are pleasant individuals to be with. Even if the others make mistake which are disturbing to them, they try to find reasons behind it and try to analyse the reasons of evil and not criticize the individual. In other words, these individuals are generally understanding and also keep patience to understand the reasons behind events. Their friends and loved ones may get irritated with them at times because when they are describing some evil person and want to get their attention and sympathy; the sevens are unable to provide that. They do not portrait another as devil and try to find the helplessness behind his evil attitude.

Generally sevens are stable and balanced and are rarely hyper excited. They are subtle individuals and have inner richness. That means, they have a sense of fulfilment and are mostly contented and happy.

Some of number sevens may be at another extreme and take life easy. They generally dislike the competitive world and like to remain aloof from that. In that process, they may not become the 'successful individuals' in the modern sense of the word. Some of them may divert to spirituality or mysticism. They can become good and successful astrologers. They may write on the ancient civilisations or just may be the story tellers.

Number seven individuals are freedom lovers and they do not like any kind of restrictions. These individuals are not vocal and rebellious against the restrictions like the number one, but they quietly suffer. They do get out of this bad situation but may harm themselves in this process.

Sevens have the enriched inner world and are happy to be on their own. They are not against the company of other people and they enjoy social ties but they need more space for themselves. For example, they need to be alone and on their own for a short while every day.

Some individuals of this number have a powerful personality and they look very attractive. An average number seven is a popular person who is trusted and loved by his/her entourage. This is their karmic personality to attract people due to their completeness, of course in a varying degree. Due to this, sometimes, they become the target of other people's envy.

The number seven individuals are generally articulate and love to express themselves. But they are not the ones who will speak on anything and everything. Usually their loving subjects are subtle and philosophical. These individuals are usually bored with a conversation on economy and business. But they actively participate on discussions of social change and social values.

Number seven in the family

Number seven are loved in the family. Children love a number seven parent because they bring peace in the family, they are not angry at children and have lot of patience. Unlike number six, the sevens do not ask too many questions.

Children of number seven are also quiet and calm but make a problem for parents who are 'success oriented' in the modern competitive world. Since they are subtle individuals and they do not believe in the superficial worldly success, it is difficult for the parents to orient them towards competitive behaviour. As a parent, you should realise that and give them space to decide on their own.

With a companion or a friend of number seven, the individuals of other numbers should not impose their views. Since sevens are good natured and patient, they do not oppose the impositions but suffer due to it.

Health of number seven

Because of being contended and subtle, number seven are generally healthy and also take care of their health. Some of number sevens may take to odd spiritual paths and may begin to fast or do other self punishing things and may ruin their health. Such individuals should learn from yogic wisdom which explains that the path to spirituality is through body and to get over the sensuous reality and reach the energy of the soul, one has to have a healthy and energetic body.

Companions and friends of number seven

Like number six, number seven can be suited to most numbers but they are the best friends and companions of number six. Number five and seven together do not make a practical couple and the family may suffer. Both the numbers have a bent towards spirituality. Number four can show the ground reality to number seven. However, the number fours which are materially oriented and are very worldly (in contrast to the nature lover fours) are antagonist to number seven who look for peace, seclusion and inner stillness. Always remember that the intensity of a particular number as life number depends upon the other numbers and that we will learn in the next chapter. For example a number seven, who has four times four in the birth numbers and also a four in the name number may get along very well with another number four who has seven dominant in other numbers.

Number eight is generally antagonist to seven, as seven are not very well organised like eight and many eights are business and success oriented.

Care suggestions and advices to number seven

Number seven, like number five should acquire the knowledge about spirituality from serious sources. Since these people are attracted to a spiritual path, sometimes they make the mistake by going after superficial, bragging and materialistic gurus and are disappointed in the long run. They should not trust others right away and take their time before taking a decision to follow a path of spirituality.

These individuals should make an effort to be direct and vocal for defending their rights and freedom. Think always that for asserting oneself, one does not have to be harsh. It can be done humbly and politely but by acting firmly and persistently.

The number eight

Cosmos and gods

Eight is an organisational number in the Vedic tradition. The number eight in Vedic meter is used in the form of 8+12+8 called kaakubh and another form of verses is **8**+12+**8** ushnih, which is **8**+**8**+12.

Indira is the god of cosmic organisation in the Vedic tradition. He has eight attendants who are mentioned in the Vedas as Vasus. These are earth, fire, water, wind, stars, moon, dawn and twilight.

In Vedic mathematics, number eight is also important as there are eight unique groups of three numbers each.

There are eight forms of Shiva as a protector and other eight as destructor.

In Ayurveda, the science of health and healing, there are eight kinds of diagnostic practices called Ashtavidha Pariksha or the eightfold diagnosis

The number eight is important in the Yogic tradition as there are eight steps of yoga called as Ashtanga yoga.

Derived from the Ayurveda pharmacology, the rasa theory is also used in art appreciation in the Indian tradition. There are eight rasa or expressions of various emotions called the bhava.

There are four directions in the West but in the Vedic tradition, each corner of the two directions is also considered a direction. There are eight different gods who rule these directions— east by Indra, west by Varuna, North by Kubera, south by Yama, south-east by Agni, southwest by Niruthi, northwest by Vayu and northeast by Isana. These ruling deities of the directions are the basis of the science of architecture called Vastu.

Ceremonial and ritualistic tradition

Eight in the Vedic tradition represents power, functionality and practicality. There are eight forms of power of shakti called Shridevi (wealth), Bhudevi (land), Sarasvati (wisdom), Priti (love and affection), Kirti (fame), Shanti (peace and stillness), Tushti (pleasure) and Pushti (Health).

Lakshmi is the goddess of wealth and has eight forms:
1. Aadi Lakshmi is the great goddess of wealth.
2. Dhana Lakshmi is also called Aishvarya Lakshmi and is the goddess of prosperity and

luxury)

3. Dhaanya Lakshmi is the goddess of grains or food in general.

4. Gaja Lakshmi is the goddess of livestock

5. SantanaLakshmi is the Goddess of progeny

6. Dhairya Lakshmi is the Goddess of Courage and boldness.

7. Vidya Lakshmi is the Goddess of knowledge.

8. Vijaya-Lakshmi or Jaya Lakshmi is the goddess of victory.

Various festivals related to the above described goddesses are celebrated all over India.

During worship, the total surrender to the deities is done with ashathanga pranam or the salutaion where eight parts of your body are touching the earth. These are forehead, chest, hands, knees and feet.

Persons of life number eight

The individuals of number eight are well organised and they also like to take responsibilities of organisation both at home and at work. In fact, it gives them pleasure and allows them to use their capabilities. Similarly, they tend to organise their life as well and set targets for themselves even for the major events of life. For example they plan their student life, and the time thereafter. It has one good aspect that they do not make a mess of time and events.

But the bad part of this is that they feel very frustrated if things do not fall in their framework.

Some of the number eights tend to lack flexibility. They bring rigidity in their life due to a habit of setting targets. This specially happens when there is number eight at other places also besides the life number. Imagine a person born on 8-8-1900. This person will be very strongly influenced by this number.

Due to their organisational capabilities, some number eights are very well appreciated at their work place but their junior colleagues are not very happy with them. Organisational lapses are caught immediately and the number eight boss can be quite hard. There are other number eights who feel frustrated due to a lack of good organisation in a particular place and wish to do independent work.

The individuals of number eight have good business skills and can manage very well. They become successful executives and managers. The individuals of this number generally have a desire to do their independent work. This is due to their self-confidence in their organisational capabilities. Individuals of life number eight having a support of number one in their horoscopes, end up doing their independent work and they make a success out of it.

Individual with life number eight like to eat well, enjoy life but they do all this in a well organised manner. Therefore, some of them lack spontaneity. They like certainty and surety in their lives and want to have hold on events. This leads to frustration at times. But there are other number eights who have a support of number five or seven in their horoscope and due to that they keep balance and poise.

Some number eights tend to grumble very quickly and the reasons for their complaints are generally the lack of organisation and mess they observe around them. Some of them take up social work to improve things in the world. They are very good in organising money for society or a charitable trust. There are other eights, who only change things for themselves and aim at gaining wealth in order to live a luxurious life. Thus, some use their organisational and business skills to succeed and become wealthy and change their life with that, and there are others who make use of these skills for bringing transformation in the society.

Individuals of this number are social persons and are good in making public relations. Depending upon the presence of the other numbers, a number eight individual may not make a profound and sincere friend but be an attraction of the social gatherings. These are persons who know lot of people and in a social gathering; they are receiving 'hi' and 'hallo' from every corner.

Number eight individuals as an organiser or executive may sound very strict and hard to work with. However, they are easy to impress and appease if you are a well organise and efficient worker. Number eights like the conversation to the point and precise, especially at work. But do not think that persons of this number cannot enjoy life. Since they have big social circle, they are capable of dealing with all kinds of different individuals socially. They have the basic skill of PR (public relation) and are apt in orienting their conversation according to different kinds of persons.

Number eight in the family

Number eight parents or at least one parent is very good for the familial organisation. However, if both the parents are number eight, the fights may erupt. In this situation, the children may also be victim at times as parents may impose their diverse views regarding the familial organisation and cause ambivalent in child's mind.

Number eight children are generally liked by their parents as they are well organised at school and at home. They become conscious of organisation from the very beginning. However, if the parents are messy or have other kind of confusion in their speech and household organisation, the number eight children may dislike or even suffer.

Health of number eight

The persons of this number generally like to eat well and sometimes too much eating or eating at wrong places can affect their health. Many of the number eights are too busy organising their lives and putting order everywhere and do not take time to pay attention to their health. Some of them in high positions pay more attention to their business than their health, eat big business meals and get lifestyle ailments like hyper-tension, diabetes, sleep disturbances, etc.

There are other number eights who are organisers of their lives and are rather health obsessed. They eat and drink punctually and take too much care of themselves. In this process, some of them eat or drink whatever they hear about in the media or from anyone.

Companions and friends of number eight

Number eight can be good friends and companions with number nine. They also go well with persons of number four who are materially oriented. In fact, the two of number eight generally get along well. These individuals can be friends with number three but for companionship, they may find hard to deal with these persons due to their unpredictable nature.

Companionship with number five and seven is beneficial for these people. They help bring subtlety and spirituality in their lives, whereas number eight bring organisation in the lives of number five and seven.

Care suggestions and advices to number eight

Persons of this number should also learn to relax and take things easy. They lack spontaneity and many of them are rigid in their work place. They should try to take an unplanned holiday at times to get out of their excessive systematic and organised way of living.

Those number eights who have management jobs should take special care of themselves. They should take care of their diet, do proper exercise and specially should not keep the thoughts about their work in their mind all the time. This leads to sleep disturbances in many cases. These individuals should take some spiritual path not in the sense of following a guru or so, but to develop and integrate sattva (inner peace and stillness) in their lives. Please refer to my book *Patanjali and Ayurvedic Yoga* for various simple practices to develop sattva.

The number nine

Cosmos and gods

In the Vedic tradition, there are 9 planets or navagraha upon which the Vedic astrology and astronomy is based. In Vedic astrology, it is believed that the movements and position of these planets affect the lives of individuals as well as of nations. The nine planets are: Surya (Sun), Chandra (Moon), Mangal (Mars), Budha (Mercury), Brahaspati (Jupiter), Shukra (Venus), Shani (Saturn), Rahu and Ketu. Everybody knows about seven planets, the additional two are Rahu and Ketu which represent different positions of the moon in relation to the other planets.

In the ancient literature of India, there is a repeated reference of body being a house with nine doors. This refers to the nine openings we have in our body: two nostrils, two eyes, two ears, mouth and two openings for excretion.

In the Vedas, number nine is mentioned as puranank or a complete number. It is symbolic of the cosmic creation. The nine months of the time of pregnancy is also mentioned as the completion of creation where each month is symbolic of one of the energies. The ninth month completes the creation with all the energies in perfection.

Ceremonial and ritualistic tradition

There are nine holy nights or navaratra twice a year when there is worship and celebration all over India. They fall on the rising moon of the month of chaitra (around mid March) and month of Ashwin (around mid September). The ritualistic symbolism of navaratra is to worship the nine different forms of Shakti or the cosmic power. After the autumn navratra, the tenth day is celebrated as the victory day— the victory of good over evil. Rama who represents the purity and righteousness fought with Ravana who had taken away his wife and won the war on this day. It is said that Rama was told that he will get the power to fight and win after he has completed the worship of the nine shakties or various forms of feminine cosmic powers or the goddesses.

Navratra is also the time when purification practices are recommended by Ayurveda. Scientifically, this time is the end of the two major seasons and the imbalances accumulated in the body should be thrown out by various purification practices called panchkarma. Since it is also customary to fast during navaratra, it seems like the integration of medical tradition into ritualistic tradition.

Persons of life number nine

Persons with life number 9 are generally rationalists or what we call in popular terminology as persons ruled by their mind. Many times they get into conflicts with other people because they want to have reasoning for everything. As children, they ask too many questions about how things function and why they should do what they are asked to do.

The individuals of this number are generally perfectionist. They proceed in their work with profound thinking and rationality. With these qualities, the persons of this number are able to make good researchers and scientist. However, the ones doing a routine jobs also use this ability in their own way. The intensity of this characteristic depends upon the intelligence level of an individual. Some of the number nines may use this trait in a negative sense of being excessively critical and finding faults in everything.

Number nine individuals are generally reliable because they do not like to leave things half way. Number nine is the number of completion and also creativity at subtle level. You have already seen that persons of number three have an artistic bent of mind and even if they are not in performing arts themselves, they have great attraction for aesthetics and for beautiful things.

Number nine however are performers at a bigger level. Intellectuals of this number could be good in architecture, geology and archaeology.

Number nine with a combination of number five in their chart or as their name number tend to live a life of conflict between what their mind says and what their heart says. Outwardly, they always like to have an appearance of a person of no non-sense who abide by rules and is correct and rational. However, the inner conflict develops with the influence of number five.

When number nine persons who have other dominating number seven usually have yearning for spirituality. In other words, they have a desire to explore the subtle powers of existence. Some of them may suffer from a dilemma between the world of mind they usually tend to live, which also goes well with our modern times, and their urge for the subtle and invisible power of the universe.

Some number nine may have rebellious behaviour. But this is unlike the rebellion of the persons of number one. The nines rebel if you ask them to do things or follow a path without rational explanation. One should first win the individuals of this number rationally with arguments and then proceed with them for a working relationship.

The individuals of this numbers are criticized, as well as appreciated for their uncompromising and perfectionist qualities. They are criticized by those who want to be fast. The ones who have a hectic and nervous nature also do not like this behaviour of number nine. Those individuals who have patience and leave number nine independent to do their job appreciate them very much. But at time, their critics end of appreciating them, as they realise the value of slow, steady and perfect task.

As stated above, number nine is a number of perfection and some of these individuals may have a mental state of complacency. With this trait, they may at times sound egoistic and boastful to others. But one should keep in mind that number nines are not those individuals who will boast and then not come up to the expectations. They work hard to come true to their words.

Number nine in the family

As a parent, number nine likes to have the atmosphere of reason in the family. This reminds me of an old French nursery rhyme:

Papa veut que je raisonne comme une grande personne,
Moi je dit que le bonbon vaut le mieux que le raison.

(Papa wants me to be rational like an adult. I say that a bonbon is better than reasoning).

Children of number nine are rather independent in nature. They are not strong willed or stubborn like number one persons, but they are persistent in putting their ideas into practice. They will not rebel immediately like number one, but they will not listen to their parents if they want them to do something without convincing them rationally. The kids of this number may get problems with the parents of number five or seven if they try to impose their special ideology or food habits on them.

Health of number nine

Rationality and reasoning being their basic trait, the individuals of this number take care of their health and lead disciplined lives. Unlike some number fives, they are not allured by sects or special regimens for their health and spirituality. They do not follow anybody or do anything until they are really convinced. In fact, number nine are usually against being vegetarian or vegan or following a health guru, etc., for taking care of their health. They believe in discipline and regularity in their deeds.

Some number nines rebel against all that is 'alternative' and in this process, they may harm themselves. For example they may be convinced with the norms of the modern society where our 'food is little better than poison'* and may refused to take care of their health and eat all kinds of foods. This category of number nine individuals suffers from stomach problems and other problems related to digestion.

Persons of this number may be vulnerable to get some nagging health problems like various aches and pains but they are largely related to imbalance in the body and disappear with some care and proper regimen.

Companions and friends of number nine

Number nine together with each other can go along well as friends but there are ego frictions in them as companions. Best combination for companionship and friendship is number six and four. Number nine generally needs a companion with patience. Number five and seven may get problems with number nine due to their search for subtle energy that is beyond the sensuous reality and persons of number nine may have difficulty in understanding. However, there are individuals who respect each other's views without imposing their own.

---

* This is a citation from my book: *Ayurveda Food Culture and Recipes* from the Foreword written by Professor Dharmanand Sharma.

Eight and nine persons can do very well together in business and any other kind of financial partnership. Number one persons may have difficulty with nine. Both of them may be assertive in their own way leading to friction in relationships.

Care suggestions and advices to number nine

Number nine persons generally do fine as we live in times where the world is mind oriented and not heart oriented. I suggest that the number nine person should make an effort to evoke their subtle energy. Normally number nine do not have a tendency to do that. They should convince themselves by experiencing the subtle energy that there is a power beyond the reality of the senses. People of this number are delighted with these experiences and they can describe that very well to initiate others on a spiritual path.

In many cases, the problem of the persons of this number is their dilemma between mind and heart when they take to a spiritual path. In some cases, they have dilemma between the mind and soul. This happens to those number nines who have developed intuitive capabilities from their past karma. These ones usually have number five and seven also dominating in their numbers. The strength of number nine dominates and there is confusion with the other forces. They are advised to educate themselves with serious literature. For example, I will advise them to study Yoga Sutras of Patanjali.

Chapter 3

Making your Horoscope

After having learnt to calculate your life number and the number of your name, you learnt about the characteristic qualities of each number. In this chapter, you will learn to organise this knowledge in a comprehensive way to make an entire horoscope. First thing to understand is that the individual numbers in your date of birth have also their influence besides your life number and name number, which of course have major influence. Let us take some examples. Radha was born on 22-12-2000. Besides her life number, also write down the sum of her individual numbers first:

4:3:2

Life number: 9

Name number: 5

Please recall this table to calculate the name number quickly:	
A, J and S are	1
B, K and T are	2
C, L and U are	3
D, M and V are	4
E, N and W are	5
F, O and X are	6
G, P and Y are	7
H, Q and Z are	8
I and R are	9

Numbers nine and five have major influence in Radha's life. Since Radha has four times number two, therefore she has also considerable influence of number two.

Next step is to come to the sum of the day, month and year. Here we have numbers four, three and two. The two emphasizes the previous twos and four and three have also minor influence.

For convenience, display the birth numbers on a set of two triangles. Those of you who have read my books on Ayurveda must have seen these triangles mentioned in almost every book. They represent the three energies at the physical and another set of three energies at the mental level. In between is the soul that is the cause of being. These are seven dimensions of a human being in my former literature. I take here the double triangle as a base to display numbers for a horoscope. Display the numbers occurring in the date of birth on the corners of these triangles. Wherever there are two, three or four numbers, put them as many times on the right place of the triangles.

You will have an over-view of the numbers displayed on the triangles or hexagon. This is your basic horoscope and you have to learn to see the place of the name number, as well as the day, month and year numbers to get a complete picture of a person.

Seven Dimensions of a Human Being

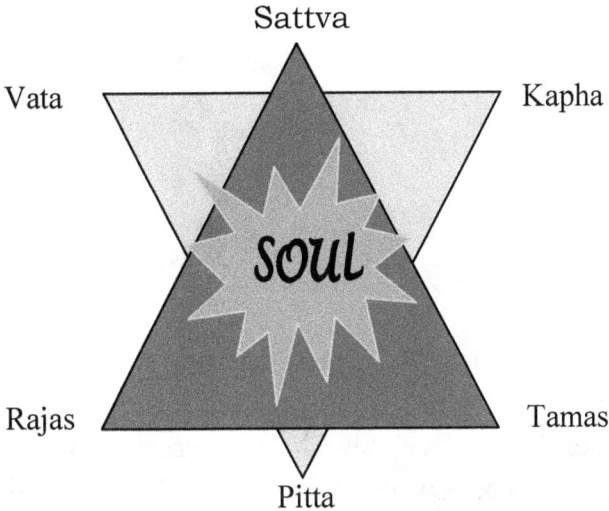

Given below are two versions of the placement of numbers for making a horoscope. The version on the left is when you are doing with handwriting and on the right is a version that you can do easily with computer and it looks better due to its three dimensional effect.

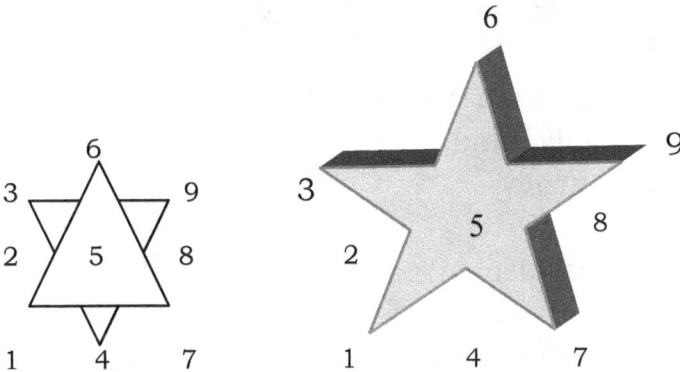

Let us display the numbers of Radha's horoscope:

2222

1

Radha has four times number two and that means despite her life number being 9 and name number being five, she has a strong influence of number two. Of course she will have all the characteristics of number nine in her basic personality but she has also a strong influence of number five. She may have conflict between her rational and mathematical vision with the mysterious and subtle energy of the universe. To put in simple words, that is the dilemma between mind and heart. Please recall that the birth number is from your past lives, the name number is from the sanskara given to you by your family and are constituted from your present karma.

Radha has also numbers three and four in the sum of her day and month. These will have periodic influence in her life. Number three may influence her to have a bent of mind towards artistic activity. The number four may lead her to have love for nature or love for material things of life. With the combination of three and four, Radha may find her artistic expression in pottery or gardening, flower arrangement. These activities relate to earth and art both. But this passion may not be long lasting.

In another case, if someone has life number three and name number four, this person is strongly oriented to the above described creative activities.

We have a situation in the example of Radha with four times number two and the number of the year is also two. Thus, this horoscope is strongly influenced by number two that makes Radha lead an eventful life. Number two is a number of happenings and life is never a straight line for the persons of this number. However, Radha has life and name numbers nine and five. Her happening will not affect her mentally so much as to a person of life number two.

Like in the above example, you will arrive at a similar situation with other numbers also where a single number repeats several times. Take an example of someone born on 4-4-1944 or 9-9-1999. Make these two horoscopes to exercise your mind.

Here are some more examples for you:

3-3-1933
Life number twenty two but the influence of number three is very strong.

5-5-1955
Life number is three but the influence of five is predominant

11-11-1911
Life number is seven but the influence of 1 is stronger than seven

You can learn to make a horoscope with regular practice. You have to learn properly the significance of each number and then learn to apply it on the given numbers in a horoscope. The skill lies in being adept in knowing what and how much influence the life number will have and the effect of the name number and the individual numbers.

Persons with multiple and unified numbers

Contrary to the above example, there are persons who have many different numbers in their horoscope. Paula has the following data:

25-5-1989
7:5:9
Life number: 3
Name number: 6

Persons with diversity of numbers possess multiple qualities. That means that they have characteristic qualities of all these numbers. However, the life number is the primary factor and the name number comes second. The other numbers influence according to their presence and they may have also a periodic influence in the life of an individual.

Let us go in details of Paula's horoscope. Her life number is three and of course first of all you should go over the qualities of number three. Paula has aesthetic orientation and her efforts are oriented to make everything look nice. If she is in performing arts, her talent is shown there. Her name number is 6 and obviously, this number also dominates in her life. That makes Paula a stable and tolerant person who is generally balanced. She may also be wavering and indecisive at times. However, in her chart, she has number five twice and that shows that she is blessed with intuitive quality. This makes her less wavering in her decisions.

Paula has number nine two times. That shows the predominance of rationality in her life. The combination of two nines and two fives may make her a person who has dilemmas between mind and heart.

Now we are left with numbers one, two and eight which will have a tiny influence on her personality and life events. They may also have periodic influence.

Seven, five and nine are her numbers of date, month and year respectively. Five and nine high lights the effect of already existing numbers is her chart. Seven has an additional influence. That provides her completeness and enhances the balancing and subtle numbers five and six. With several times five and one time seven is leading her for the search of unknown.

I am going to give you an example of horoscope where you have all the nine numbers. The person's name is Lucile or Horst which make the number of their name eight. This person was born on:
27-3-1964
9: 3: 2 are the respective numbers of the day, month and year.
The life number is 5

Let us display the birth numbers on the chart:

You see that this person has seven numbers out of nine in the date of birth. Since this person's life number is five, which has a major influence and the name number is eight, this person has all the numbers. The extra influence comes from numbers nine, three and two which are the numbers of day, month and year.

Such persons are generally multifaceted and multitalented. Some of them may have this weakness that they are unable to pay attention to a unidirectional theme and may end up becoming *Jack of all trades and master of none.* But overall, they are balanced personalities and are not the one who will lead an extreme life. Persons with very few numbers generally lead very intense life. There is no value judgement associated to intensity. For example a person born on 11.11.1911 has an extreme horoscope. Imagine if this person's name number is also one or eleven, this intensity heightens. Extreme will power and determination with unidirectional qualities, this person will lead an intense life. He could be a great scholar always buried in books. Another of this horoscope may be a very successful thief or a dacoit.

One should keep in mind that when there is repeatedly one number, like in the above case, the influence of this number is even more intense than the life and the name numbers. Here are some examples:

4-4-1944
Life number is 8
But the influence of number four is stronger than even the life number

9-9-1999
Life number is one but the influence of number nine is stronger than the life number.

Making different horoscopes

If you want to sharpen your ability in numerology and learn to make horoscopes, pay attention to the following three steps:

1. A mathematical practice of making horoscopes of different people with diverse numbers and diverse professions.
2. Interpretations of the numbers you get from diverse persons and learn to correlate all these numbers.

3. According to the Vedic tradition, to enhance any ability to a higher level, one needs to develop intuitive power. One needs to evoke the subtle energy which lies unused in all of us. So develop your own intuitive power which will help you to correlate easily the influence of different numbers and see the relationship between the subtle and the practical aspects of life. I recommend my book *Aum: The Infinite Energy* that describes simple practices of yoga and pranayama to develop inner human power.

Flowers of Ashoka. The word Ashoka means the one without sorrow.

Chapter 4

Periods of Change and Turmoil

This chapter will help you calculate the periods of turmoil and intense change in your life. Please recall that my message is to use astrology to guide you and not be superstitious and fearful with the events to come or to dwell upon the past with regret. The period of turmoil and change is a hard period of life but not necessarily negative. Howsoever terrible, hard and intolerable this period may be, it carries some hidden positive energy for the future. This period is like autumn but there is always a spring afterwards. The fallen leaves make place for new leaves. The principal message for this time of your life is to stay calm and to delay taking major decisions or taking up new projects. Be modest and humble during this period and do not lose your calm. Exercise this attitude of— *take life as it comes*. Accept the upheavals with calmness and with the attitude that we human beings cannot control everything. It is suggested to use some kind of yogic and meditative practices for attaining stillness of mind.

The purpose of this knowledge is to prepare you for managing your life better. There are certain major things one keeps postponing in one's life. By knowing about the smooth and turbulent periods of your life, you can be inspired to take major decisions and begin important projects during your smooth period. On the other hand, avoid the disturbed period to do all this.

Calculations

For calculating this period of turmoil and changes, calculate your life number first with your date of birth as described in Chapter 1. For example your date of birth is:

23-9-1989
Your life number is: 5

Then take the sum total of your age. When your life number and a total number of your age coordinate with each other, you have this period of major changes in your life. In the present example, this period will be at the age of 5, 14, 23, 32, 41, 50, 59, 68, 77, 86, and so on. According to the Vedic numerology, your fifth year begins after your fourth birthday. That means, the influence of this number begins gradually at this time and is at a peak when you are five or the sum of your age number is five. The effect gradually descends after your birthday and comes down slowly during the following months. That means it ends before your sixth birthday.

During this period, you may feel perplexed and without direction. You may part with certain relationships or loved ones, and so on. Or else, you may see too much confusion around you and you may find yourself overburdened with various situations and happenings. At times you may feel that you cannot take it anymore or you cannot handle this turmoil

Let us take some more examples in order to understand this number puzzle better.

Date of birth: 09-09-1987
Life number of this person is 7.

At the age of 7, 16, 25, 34 and so on (every nine years), this person is affected by some disturbances in his/her life. This is a natural process in life and affects all people. This period can be compared to shifting from one house to another. That involves lot of work, effort and disturbance, but ultimately one feels better. It gives us a chance to throw away the unneeded accumulated goods. One gets more space for oneself and less oppression from one's surroundings. However, these feelings of comfort come much later than the disturbances we face while sorting out, packing and unpacking. Similarly, the good effects of this period of turmoil are felt only later after some lapse of time.

Life has both pain and joy. Generally people compare the period of pain to the darkness of a night and say that during this time, one should wait for the light. We human being are greedy for joy and do not want to accept the painful period of life. There are so many people in this world who keep remembering the "joy they had" and waste so much of their time dwelling in the past. They grumble that why the good days are gone. If we inculcate the wisdom that pain and joy are an integral part of life and none of them stay forever, we are able to go through life with ease. Life is ever changing and dynamic and we should accept events as they unfold. The wisdom of the present calculation about the disturbed period should provide you a guide line and help you to prepare for this period.

Actually, no period of life is totally negative or painful. There are happenings which may outwardly seem negative but in the long run they bring some fruitful results. During the above described period of turmoil, you may part with your girl friend or boy friend. You may feel pained and may suffer from the loss. To forget that pain, you may go to a far away land and have there the greatest time of your life. Or else you may meet a partner whom you may find 'just perfect'. At this moment, the parting from the previous relationship may seem to you as a stroke of good luck that opened new avenues in your life.

Everything is fluid and gradual in nature. Events of life are not abrupt and they happen when it is time for them to happen. One thing leads to another and what is happening at present is an accumulated affect of karma from present and past lives. The past is not in our hands but the present is. Therefore, the purpose is how we can make the best out of what we already have. For making the best of effort to go through the periodic disturbed periods of life, we need to build our inner strength. According to the Vedic tradition, the inner strength comes to us from the energy of soul. To evoke this energy, one has to learn to silence one's mind. That means one has to withdraw the senses temporarily and break the chain of thoughts. The mind which is always busy and indulgent with the senses and the external world achieves a state of silence and attain oneness with the soul. Thus, one should do yogic concentration practices regularly to build up inner strength and stillness. This helps us to go through joys and perils of life with stability. This is also the principal teaching of the ancient scriptures to keep stability of mind in joyous and painful situations of life. Just like death is as much a reality of life as the birth, similarly, pain is as much a part of life as joy and happiness. Only thing is that we do not grumble when we have joy but many of us constantly grumble and indulge into self-pity, when we have to face the disturbed and difficult situations of life.

Planning for the disturbed period

Being aware of the disturbed and smooth periods of life, we can plan our life better. For example keeping this calculation in mind, we can decide to undertake our new project before or after this period and not during.

Many of you may be doing some concentration or meditative practices everyday but during this period, you should enhance these for your peace of mind. Pranayama or the controlled breathing exercises from yoga help stabilise the mind and enhance power of concentration and insight. These help to take right decision at right time. Do the breathing exercises by sending the prana or breathe to your navel point. Imagine your life number there and hold the breath. Gradually release the breath. Do this exercise whenever you feel helpless due to various situations during this period. You will get a feeling of instant relief.

You should particularly pay attention to take thoughtful decisions during this period. Never decide anything in haste. When you are about to decide, tell yourself to take some more time. The disturbed period of your horoscope is a challenging time that provides you an opportunity for your inner development. You come out of it as more courageous and more learned person. Therefore, do not take this as punishment.

In Vedic thinking, we believe that our joys and pains are karmic and we ourselves are responsible for them. We must accept both in equal stride and resolve to do such karma that we are able to lessen the pain not yet come. The aim of the numerological prediction of this period is to be well organised and prepared to deal with life better.

Chapter 5

Your Lucky Numbers

Besides making horoscope and predicting various things, you should also learn how to make numbers influence your daily life. The most important is that you should know about the significance of numbers. If you have learnt well the significance of individual numbers and have practiced in making various horoscopes as described in the last chapter, you will be able to easily learn about the selection of numbers for various events.

Fundamentally, your life number is your lucky number. Your name number is your second lucky number. The dates and time pertaining to these numbers are your lucky dates. However, there are events that you want to lessen the effect of your own number in a particular situation. For example your life number is one and your name number is also one. You are in a situation where you need to be humble and not so assertive in order to have a 'yes' from someone or to win somebody's heart. In that case you do not wish to emphasize your number one traits. In such a situation, it is better to chose number five, six or seven for date and time and if you can chose a day, it should be Friday.

Taking the same example of number one, in another situation, you have to be very assertive and have to convince the others in a meeting with your strong arguments. In this case, you have to emphasize your number one qualities. Dates like one, ten, nineteen and twenty eight would be lucky for you. Use the same trick with time and the best day would be Monday.

However, we cannot decide all the time dates, times and days. But the idea of this knowledge is that you can use it wherever you can. For personal events, we can generally decide that. A business person can decide his/her dates for major meetings and decisions. We can decide date and time for beginning a new project, entering into new house, beginning renovation or construction, and so on.

Personally, I decide the number of chapters of my books based on Vedic numerology. I also deicide the number of pages of my books for English version but in various translations the number changes.

Let us take another example. Number two is eventful and a lot happens with the persons of this number. To emphasize and highlight the decisive characteristics needed for a life situation, they can chose number one as date and time. For peace, harmony and stability, they can choose seven.

Persons with life number eight or nine can chose seven for a decision which concerns more heart than mind. Similarly, the number fives and sevens can chose number eight for business meetings and number nine for those events where they need their mind more than heart.

In Vedic numerology, we also lay a great emphasis on the days of the moon calendar. The lucky days are of rising moon for major deeds or for beginning new projects. We always sow seeds in the rising sun, which is before noon. The Indian farmers are very particular to sow certain seeds on specific days. For example, in my region in the Himalayas, the pumpkin seeds are sowed in *Maha Shivaratri*. That is the great Shiva's night when he wakes up from his meditation in spring.

The good beginning

The lucky numbers are also chosen for various deeds specifically. For beginning a new project or laying a foundation stone of the house, or signing a new contract, one is the lucky number. It is suggested to do a little ceremony by some concentration practices on Monday at 10 in the morning. Number one gives you input for determination to complete the project.

For a writer to begin a new project for a book, the suggested day is Thursday. For proposing someone or expressing one's love, Friday is suggested at a chosen time of four, five or seven. Same is true for deciding a wedding date.

For a party to celebrate something, chose nine which is a complete and highest number and denotes your fulfilment and happiness. For beginning a new job, chose Monday or Thursday and with dates of number eight or nine. For your art exhibition, or a new art work, chose number three as time or date. However, if you wish to sell art works, chose number eight. For learning programmes related to spirituality and development of your inner being, think of choosing number five or seven.

If you are helping two people to solve a dispute or it is your own dispute with someone and you wish to resolve it, chose number six for date and time of the meeting. Remember that number six is for balance and harmony. Number six also emphasizes our own inner balance while we are in a dispute for one reason or the other. If you are having a talk to resolve dispute with your partner, chose six in combination with Friday.

Numbers and your attention

It is important to pay attention to numbers. In the Vedic tradition, there are both sun and moon calendars and the significance of the days is described. Special significance is given to the first day of the month in both the calendars. Full moon and new moon are other two important days. I recently wrote on my facebook page: 'Happy month of September for all of you'. May be I surprised many of you. Everybody celebrates the beginning of the year with such fervour, then why not the first day of the month? The importance given to the numbers in the Vedic tradition is to make people conscious of the time and finally of their life. Living in an aware manner leads to a better concentration and better memory. It helps filter some the worldly non-sense that we do not require but go on with it due to a herd instinct. The essence is that when we get rid of the cover of darkness (tamas) from around our soul, we come to a state of pure energy and we cannot do anything wrong in that enlightened state.

।। बि म्भे दे व

बि म्भुं देवासे

णवकोन: म्

रिथि श्री सूर

सरस्वती ।

वाक्: १ सु

Conclusion

There is a relationship of numbers in the context of space and time. Although in different countries there are diverse calendars of time calculations, but we have chosen the modern Christian era calendar as it is being used internationally and for international events. During the last century, we had numbers one and nine. Century number is one. Nine speaks for rationality and research and development. One signifies determination and will. This later, when used negatively, result in disaster. The two world wars happened in this century. Research and development in telecommunication touched its peak. Similarly, better and efficient aviation was developed. With the result of all this, the time and space have developed another dimension and our globe has become like a village. We enter into the century of number two and there are endless happenings and events. Internet has changed our lives. But this was developed during last century. An easy and free access to knowledge has brought out everything in open. The rulers cannot hide their sins, waiting to be discovered after their deaths. Wikileaks brought everything in open. Similarly the sex scandals of many leaders came to light and all that was possible with the development of finest of instruments.

The present century with all its advantages is still shaking the world. Everybody, from a little child of five to an old person, is saying, 'I am busy'. Time has acquired another dimension in our lives. We have become economical in time on the one hand and on the other, nobody has time. This is a state of turmoil.

The turmoil does not only end here. There is a commotion within our body and mind. Everything is fast and so is the process of making money for many. Politicians and business owners have limitless greed. The public is gradually poisoned with air, water, food and the nature is being destroyed. All this is resulting in numerous disorders. Their treatment leads to another business of insurances and medical industry. The holy profession of healing has been converted into a wretched business which is leading to misery to a larger section of the society almost everywhere in the world.

Advice for this Century

It is even more essential than before to have a spiritual way during present times. Please do not confuse spirituality with religion. Though all religions advise for spirituality and show one path or the other for inner peace and harmony, but they also impose many restrictions and boundaries which many of you may not accept. Therefore the religion-neutral spirituality is a path for everybody. The essence of spirituality is to stop the new knowledge from the senses in order to silence the mind. Once the mind is still and is no more involved with the senses or with the worldly activities, it comes closer to the soul, which is our cause of being. An individual soul is a part of the Universal Soul and when we reach the energy of the soul, we are closer to self-realisation. That means our real self is soul with endless energy and we realise this fact. This opens a way for us to intuitive and subtle wisdom which is beyond the sensuous knowledge.

About the Author

Along with a doctorate degree in reproduction biology in India, Dr. Verma studied Neurobiology in Paris University and obtained a second doctorate. She pursued advanced research at the National Institutes of Health, Bethesda (USA) and the Max-Planck Institute in Freiburg, Germany. At the peak of her career in medical research in a pharmaceutical company in Germany, she realised that the modern approach to health care is basically fragmented and non-holistic. Besides, we are directing all our efforts and resources to cure disease rather than maintaining health. In response, Dr. Verma founded The New Way Health Organisation (NOW) in 1986 to spread the message of holistic living, preventive methods for health care and to promote the use of mild medicine and various self-help therapeutic measures.

Dr. Verma grew up with a strong familial tradition of Ayurveda with a grandmother who had enormous Ayurvedic wisdom and was a gifted healer. She has studied Ayurveda in the traditional Guru-shishya style with Acharya Priya Vrat Sharma of the Benares Hindu University for 23 years.

Dr. Verma is an ardent researcher and is working hard to compile the living tradition of Ayurveda and spread it in the world through her books and other activities. She has published twenty three books on yoga, Ayurveda, Women and Companionship. The books are published in various languages of the world. Besides, she has published numerous scientific articles. Several other books are in preparation. She lectures extensively, teaches in Europe for several months a year, trains students at her two centres in India and gives radio and television programmes. A film on Ayurveda with her was made by German television in 1995 and was shown in 100 countries, in 130 languages. It was the first film on Ayurveda.

Dr. Verma has founded Charaka School of Ayurveda to train interested people with genuine Ayurvedic education so that they can further impart the knowledge of Ayurvedic way of life and save people from becoming a victim of charlatanry in Ayurveda. She is doing several research projects on medicinal plants and their combination in the form of remedies. She is the founder and chairperson of *The Ayurveda Health Organisation*, which is a charitable trust for distributing and promoting

Numerology: Based on the Vedic Tradition

Ayurvedic remedies and yoga therapy in rural areas of India. She does regular lectures and workshops for school children in the rural and remote areas of the Himalayas to promote wisdom of traditional science and medicine. Dr. Verma gives seminars, lectures and teaches in the *Charaka School of Ayurveda* with guru-shishya tradition.

For more information and contacts for Dr. Verma's school and teaching programme see www.ayurvedavv.com and www.drvinodverma.com

Dr. Vinod Verma's Publications

1. *Patanjali's Yoga Sutra: A Scientific Exposition* (Published in English, Hindi and German).
2. *Ayurveda for Inner Harmony: Nutrition, Sexual Energy and Healing* (Published in English, German, Italian, French, Romanian and Hindi).
3. *Ayurveda a Way of Life* (Published in English, German, Italian, French, Spanish, Czech, Greek, Portuguese, Slovenian and Hindi).
4. *The Kamasutra for Women* (Published in English [America and India], German, French, Dutch, Romanian, Italian, Portuguese, Slovenian Hindi and Malayalam).
5. *Stress-free Work with Yoga and Ayurveda* (Published in German, English [America and India] and Hindi).
6. *Patanjali and Ayurvedic Yoga* (Published in English, German and Hindi).
7. *Programming Your Life with Ayurveda* (Published in German, French, English, Slovenian and Czech).
8. *Ayurvedic Food Culture and Recipes* (Published in English, German, Czech and Hindi).
9. *Yoga: A Natural Way of Being* (Published in English, German, French, Italian and Hindi).
10. *Companionship and Sexuality (Based on Ayurveda and the Hindu tradition)* (Published in English and German).
11. *Natural Glamour: The Ayurveda Beauty Book* (Published in German, Spanish and English)
12. *Losing and Maintaining Weight with Ayurveda and Yoga* (Published in English, Slovenian and German).
13. *The Timeless Wisdom of Ayurveda: A Scientific Exposition* (Published in English and German)

136

14. *Prakriti and Pulse: The Two Mysteries of Ayurveda* (Published in German)
15. *Good Food for Dogs: Vegetarian nourishment based on Ayurvedic wisdom* (Published in German and English)
16. *Diet for Losing Weight* (published in German and English)
17. *Aum: The Infinite Energy* (Published in German and English)
18. *Pulse Diagnose in Chinese and Ayurvedic Medicine* (co-author for TCM Dr. Florian Ploberger) (published in German)
19. *Shiva's Secrets for Health and Longevity* (published in German and English)
20. *Healing Hands: The Ayurvedic Massage workbook* (published in English)
21. *Prevention of Dementia* (published in German and English)
22. *Ayurveda for Dogs* (published in German and English)
23. Numerology: Based on the Vedic Tradition (published in English)
24. Ayurvedic Cuisine: God's own Apothecary— Simple Healing Remedies from Ayurvedic Herbs and Spices (in preparation)

The Charaka School of Ayurveda and Patanjali Yogadarshana Society (Himalayan Centre)

The Charka School of Ayurveda (CSA) has been founded by Dr. Vinod Verma to spread the genuine classical tradition as well as the living tradition of Ayurveda in the world for promoting healthy living and preventing ailments. Its aim is to teach people a healthy lifestyle which enhances immunity and vitality and enables them to live a life with an optimum level of energy. For minor ailments, people should be capable of using home remedies, appropriate physical and mental exercises and nutrition.

CSA aims to bring genuine and practical aspects of Ayurveda to people and save them from Americanised and Europeanised distorted versions of Ayurveda and other forms of charlatanry that do more harm than good.

To achieve this purpose, CSA organises to train students in Europe who can further spread the message of Ayurvedic lifestyle and help people with genuine massages, purification practices, nutrition and other practical aspects of Ayurveda. The school is in association with the most learned persons of Ayurveda in India and several exclusive persons involved in health education in Europe.

The object of Patanjali Yogadarshana Society is to spread the message of Patanjali in the world. The wisdom of the Yoga Sutras is not only beneficial for the yogis but also for our day-to-day normal life. Its aim is to enhance *sattva* or the inner stillness and peace in the world as well as in the individual minds. With years of research on Yoga and Ayurveda, Dr. Verma has founded the Ayurvedic Yoga and has written a book on the subject.

Himalayan Centre

Lectures, Seminars and Training Programmes

To get detailed information on the Charaka School of Ayurveda as well as our other programmes in India and Europe, visit our website or contact us by email.

The New Way Health Organisation .NOW. A-130, Sector 26, Noida 201301, U.P.,

India

Tel. 0091 (0)120 2527820 or
(0) 9873704205 or (0)9412224820
www.ayurvedavv.com
www.drvinodverma.com
Contact at: ayurvedavv@yahoo.com

www.ingramcontent.com/pod-product-compliance
Lightning Source LLC
Chambersburg PA
CBHW052208270326
41931CB00011B/2265